CROSSING THRESHOLDS

CROSSING THRESHOLDS

The Making and Remaking
of a 21st-Century College Chaplain

Lucy A. Forster-Smith

Foreword by
Martin B. Copenhaver

CASCADE *Books* • Eugene, Oregon

CROSSING THRESHOLDS
The Making and Remaking of a 21st-Century College Chaplain

Copyright © 2015 Lucy A. Forster-Smith. All rights reserved. Except for brief quotations in critical publications or reviews, no part of this book may be reproduced in any manner without prior written permission from the publisher. Write: Permissions. Wipf and Stock Publishers, 199 W. 8th Ave., Suite 3, Eugene, OR 97401.

Cascade Books
An Imprint of Wipf and Stock Publishers
199 W. 8th Ave., Suite 3
Eugene, OR 97401

www.wipfandstock.com

ISBN 13: 978-1-62564-132-8.

Cataloguing-in-Publication Data

Forster-Smith, Lucy A.

Crossing thresholds : the making and remaking of a 21st-century college chaplain / Lucy A. Forster-Smith.

xviii + 142 p. ; 23 cm. Includes bibliographical references.

ISBN 13: 978-1-62564-132-8.

1. College chaplains—United States. 2. College chaplains—biography. 3. Church work with students. I. Title.

BV4376 .F20 2015

Manufactured in the U.S.A.   08/07/2015

To: Tom, Chris, Mara, and Anna, my sun, moon, and stars

"What's lost is nothing to what's found, and all the death that ever was, set next to life, would scarcely fill a cup."

—FREDERICK BUECHNER, *GODRIC*

Contents

Foreword

LUCY FORSTER-SMITH CONFESSES EARLY on in this remarkable memoir that the role of college chaplain is "riddled with ambiguity." I'll say.

At Macalester College, where Lucy served as college chaplain for twenty years, she was placed in a prominent role at key ceremonial occasions—for instance, offering a prayer at the beginning of the school year and at graduation—but her office was tucked away in a basement where it could be easily ignored. Lucy writes that the chaplain's job "is to see the campus from the outside while also engaging the inner life of its members. We need to be inside and outside at the same time." Only a wise and seasoned college chaplain could capture this ambiguity in words. Only a truly remarkable chaplain, like Lucy Forster-Smith, could also come to embrace such an ambiguity.

A member of one congregation I served reflected, "The Christian church is a remarkable thing—we hire someone to tell us things we don't fully believe and don't really want to hear." This ambiguity is only heightened in the case of college chaplaincy, because the one doing the hiring is a secular institution. The ambiguity is heightened even further in Lucy's case because Macalester is one of the top-ranked colleges in a national survey for "ignoring God on a regular basis," a distinction many associated with the college point to with pride. Nonetheless, they want to have a chaplain.

Having a chaplain in a college like Macalester is more than an accommodation of some quirky artifact from the past, the way a school might allow a chapter of the the Flat Earth Society on their campus. Real ministry happens in such a setting—if the chaplain is skilled, patient, and responsive, as clearly Lucy is. In Marilynne Robinson's Pulitzer Prize-winning novel, *Gilead*, Pastor Ames reflects, "That's the strangest thing about this life, about being in the ministry. People change the subject when they see you coming. And then sometimes those same people come into your study and tell you the most remarkable things."

Sometimes "ignoring God on a regular basis" just doesn't seem so compelling. Or even possible. At such times students and others seek out Lucy to tell her the most remarkable things. There is the student who is angry that there is a cross atop the chapel because not everyone on campus is a Christian. His initial expression of anger becomes the beginning of a searching conversation, and deepening relationship, over a number of years. Another student whose experience of awe in a biology lab becomes something of an epiphany, wonders who she can tell without coming across as crazy. Surely, she can't tell her professor. So she tells Lucy, and eventually, at Lucy's encouragement, she finds courage to tell the professor as well. One student comes to Lucy in desperation because his girlfriend was distraught and now is missing. When something like that happens, the chaplain's ministry is to an individual, to be sure, but also to the entire campus community. For a moment, at least, a gaping need overwhelms skepticism. At such times, no one has much energy for ignoring God anymore. A skilled chaplain steps in, in Lucy's words, "to try to provide anchors, if not answers, in moments of trauma."

In these and other instances, Lucy demonstrates what she describes as her philosophy of college chaplaincy: "Holy hospitality, that's what my vision for chaplaincy is about. Holding the door open, inviting others to cross the religious threshold that awaits them . . . Especially during the college years when the spiritual may get pushed to the edges, what I mean by holy hospitality is a way of holding the door of the heart open."

Another of Lucy's descriptions of her work is "guerrilla chaplaincy." Borrowing the phrase from the "guerrilla theater" movement, she affirms the value of surprise for the way it can help us reexamine assumptions about our lives. Many people are initially put off by the unexpected. Lucy sees it as an opening, an opportunity: "Sometimes I feel like the best thing I can do as a chaplain is to encourage moments of insight and wonder on my campus, that the best kind of 'guerilla chaplaincy' I can muster, is just to expect holy surprise in my own life and to encourage the same expectation in others."

Lucy's openness to surprise is hard won. She finds it surprising, as does the reader, that the church where she was raped as a young woman becomes, through the care of a pastor and congregation, the very same church she joins and where she is ordained to ministry. She writes with wonder: "In the weeks and months after the rape, would I have ever dreamed that I would join the very church where it occurred? Would I have even fleetingly have considered being ordained in the church sanctuary not fifty steps from the place where I thought I would die? Though I had made the decisions that had brought me here, I couldn't help but feel humbled by God's hand in this extraordinary turn of events."

It is telling that the word *surprise* pops up frequently in Lucy's narrative. Clearly, out of her own experience of life and ministry, she has come to believe that surprise is one of God's preferred ways of getting our attention.

It is also telling that the other words that recur throughout her story are *privilege* and *grateful*. Even if Lucy never used those words, however, the reader would know they are apt descriptions of her approach to her ministry. Her story veritably glows with gratitude—not in a naïve or surface way, but with the deep glow of someone who is living and working within the sweet spot of her call. As novelist and preacher Frederick Buechner famously observed, "The place God calls you to is the place where your deep gladness and the world's deep hunger meet." It is a privilege—and often downright thrilling—to be in the presence of someone who lives and works at such an intersection. That is one reason, among others, why you will love spending time with Lucy Forster-Smith through this memoir.

Martin B. Copenhaver
President, Andover Newton Theological School

Acknowledgments

THIS BOOK WOULD NOT have arrived in the reader's hands without the steady support of family, colleagues, supervisors, friends and particularly the Lilly Endowment. It is a with a debt of gratitude that I thank Chris Coble and Craig Dykstra at the Lilly Endowment for their patience, vision, care, and support. To Chris Coble for believing in the project, offering great counsel and keeping me on task. To Craig Dykstra for amazingly clarifying conversations about the work and the vocation of those of us whose practice of ministry leads us into the arena of higher education. The robust energy of religious leaders like Craig and Chris steady so many chaplains in the rocky twenty-first century.

I thank Macalester College, particularly Laurie Hamre, Brian Rosenberg, Eily Marlow, Barry Cytron, K. P. Hong, the faculty women's writing group, and many, many others, who supported me as I took to the pen.

I am so grateful to one of the most remarkable mentors I know, Sharon Daloz Parks, who was the consultant to this project. Her wise guidance, her gift of grace that often came just in the nick of time, her encouragement to tell my whole story, including the tough moments, and her belief in the role of chaplains to engage big questions and dreams worthy of a lifetime has inspired me each time I have come to the keyboard.

I thank *my* college chaplain, Larry R. Bowden, who one day in a chance conversation spoke words that set me on a course toward being a college chaplain.

For Jack and Barbara Van Ark Wilson, my pastoral godparents, who were there in the aftermath of one of scariest moments of my life and who loved me as I healed and invited me into the adventure of being a Presbyterian minister.

Acknowledgments

For Dr. Jim Loder, whose brilliance, passion, fearlessness, and deep knowledge of God's Spirit of healing and bounty guided me from the dark valley of fear to the spacious horizon of joy by his counsel and light.

For the brilliant Kate Daloz, editor, advisor, writing guide, and unflappable supporter, who read draft after draft with exacting eye and compassionate commitment to this project.

I thank the students, faculty, administrative colleagues, and chaplain friends who are present in this book. For your bold awakening to this complicated world and for the way you have given me the gift of joining you on a pilgrimage of grace and formation, I stand in awe.

And most of all, for my family, Tom, my spouse, and our children, Christopher, Mara, and Anna, who know the subtext of this book, the fear, the uncertainty, the excitement, the wonder. When I once had the opportunity to meet Frederick Buechner some years ago, I asked for his advice about writing a book. His only word to me was that I bear in mind the ones to whom the story is directed. I promptly came back home to Minnesota and put a photo of my three children on my desk. I have written this book so that my children and their children will know the world that I have had the privilege of inhabiting.

Introduction

A FEW YEARS AGO I found myself in my kitchen baking bread with a former student. After graduation from Macalester College, Jenna had ventured away from Minnesota to work as an advocate for human rights in Cyprus. Several years later she returned to the East Coast to teach English Language Learning skills to those being trained to work with immigrants—now she was back in the Twin Cities interviewing for a position at a human rights organization.

As we spoke that afternoon, Jenna reminded me of how far she had journeyed from a heart-rending tragedy that she had experienced while at Macalester. She was simply brimming with life as she described an interaction with an ELL student who had just passed the United States Citizenship test. Kneading flour into the dough, Jenna paused and then said to me, "I can't believe the way my life has evolved. When I went through all that in college I never dreamed I would be able to help others who experience tough things in their lives." I stopped my own kneading and turned to look at her. She said she sometimes felt as though she had been guided into the encounters she experienced in her work. She stopped kneading and looked at me. "I think it's a God thing. Lucy, you get it."

She was right. I did get it. I stood with flour on my hands and gratitude in my heart for this young woman. I also could almost see in her eyes the winking love of God, who steps over thresholds and accompanies us through life. That afternoon in this remarkable brimming moment, I felt so lucky to witness the ways Jenna's healing and grace had led her toward a life of joyful engagement.

In my work as a college chaplain, amid the communities of students, faculty, and staff, as well as in the church communities to which I have belonged through the years, I stand as a witness to many "God things." My role takes me into privileged territory with young adults. I see up close the spiritual hunger of this generation of young adults. Though this generation is often derided as the "nones"—that is, those who claim no religious tradition—in fact some 70 percent of them believe in God or a higher power. The young people I encounter wonder about the meaning and purpose of their lives and think deeply about how they might live out their passion to change the world. Together, we often explore the grief and loss that is so prevalent in this generation's experience. Much of my work on campus is to be a mentor, a guide, someone who can think of nothing more gratifying than to simply get to know students, who does not demand anything from them, who is not grading or assessing them but who simply appreciates their stories, laughs a lot and also weeps with them. The dreams and questions of college or university students are my habitation. These young people are not only the inheritors of the world; they are participants in shaping the world. My work with them dwells on the threshold between past and future, between receiving and launching, between preparing global citizens and watching them flourish across the planet. I have the privilege to walk with them through these crucial transitional years and often find myself profoundly moved by what shows up as we move across the vast terrain of imagination and heart.

As it does for the students I work with, a "God thing" arrives for me when I am led to a threshold place, a place of transition, a place where the reliable assumptions that have shaped my world for days or centuries no longer seem to hold out promise or hold back the pain that may be on the other side. My own journey from childhood through young adulthood and into a very gratifying profession as a chaplain in higher education has been punctuated with God things as well. A very long time ago I was a young adult trying to find my way to what I then called "God's purpose for my life." I dreamed of being a theology professor and was following that ambition when my life was derailed by a stranger's act of violence. It was in the process of healing from that traumatic personal experience that I realized my work would be to attend to the lives of young people who are at a crossroads. What better place to do this work than a college or university campus?

This book is about the way my life has been shaped and formed by the practice of ministry on campus and how my vocation has been informed by my interaction with remarkable young adults on a journey, awakened by an unexpected set of circumstances that led me squarely into work with young adults, guided by the steady steps of mentors, and held by the abundant grace of God. I hope this book will be a resource for those considering college or university chaplaincy—for people like Karl, who came to my office one sunny spring afternoon in 2006. Karl was a senior, ready to graduate from Macalester. His four years at the college had taken him from the music department, where he was an accomplished trumpeter, to the soccer field, to Ethiopia for study abroad, to doing an honors project in his chosen major, the math department. He had participated in a program I helped launch his first year and since then was involved with various religious life activities at the college, including the weekly Christian worship service.

Karl was uncharacteristically tentative that day as he began what he described as "Lucy check-in time." Sensing he had something important to share and knowing from experience that the best invitation is often the simplest, I said, "What's up?"

"Lucy, you might find this surprising but I think I want to be a college chaplain." His eyes avoided mine. "I don't know . . . I have loved, loved, loved my time here in the chapel. Vespers is so great. I watch you and how you seem to laugh so much, kind of bubble over with joy when you are with students." He continued, "If I want to be a chaplain, how do I know how to go about it? I mean, I have watched you do your thing and it seems so natural, so easy, but I think it isn't. Are there books written about what college chaplains do?" I would have normally handed him a list of books but his question confirmed what I already knew. There are few books written for those who want to be a chaplain in higher education. When I was in seminary, more than twenty-five years before, a professor handed me a copy of Princeton University chaplain Ernest Gordon's book, *Meet Me at the Door*. Since then, there have been books on parish ministry galore alongside how-to books on campus ministry. But I realized there were few resources from contemporary chaplains about who we are and how we think about the work we do.

Two years after my conversation with Karl, I approached Dr. Christopher Coble, at the Lilly Endowment to see if he had an idea where I might find funds to take a sabbatical and write such a resource, based on the years I have spent as a minister in higher education. The Lilly Endowment had funded Macalester College's Program for the Theological Exploration of Vocation, of which I was one of the Project Directors. I had served on a national advisory panel for the Program as well. I told Chris about conversations with students who wanted to take up a career as a college chaplain and how I struggled to find resources. I mentioned to him that I had run by trusted colleagues the idea of writing a book and the unanimous response had been, "Go for it!" I was excited to devote a year or more crafting a memoir-type book on my experiences.

As we talked, Chris Coble not only was taken with this idea, a *portrait* of my experience, he encouraged me to consider working on two books. The second would be a *landscape* view of chaplaincy, an edited volume of essays from chaplains across the country. He took the proposal to Dr. Craig Dykstra, then President of the Endowment's Religion Division. He was very supportive. The book you are holding is the portrait. The other book, the landscape, *College and University Chaplaincy in the 21st Century: A Multifaith Look at the Practice of Ministry on Campuses Across America,* was published by SkyLight Paths Press in 2013.

This book draws from thirty-five years of my experience in four different ministry settings. The experiences and interactions in this volume are true but I've concealed identifiers throughout.

At the heart of this book is the deep conviction that the most remarkable work I can do as a college chaplain is to encourage a new generation of young adults like Karl and Jenna to step into adulthood with intelligence, imagination and ready hearts to serve the emerging needs of God's beloved ones. And it is my deepest desire that this book will speak to you, the reader, as you encounter the joy of a college chaplain's work and the remarkable grace-filled journey that finds God at the threshold in untold ways.

CHAPTER 1

Beginnings

T HE BAGPIPES ARE TUNING up. In my pocket is a folded prayer. In my
line of vision, there is a line of students and parents snaking around the
side of the gym, waiting to enter. A teary mother holds her daughter's hand,
the daughter's face flushed with—what? Worry? Embarrassment? Fear? In
my hand is the program for the new student convocation. I check the order
of speakers as if for the first time, though it's been many autumns now that
I've stepped through the gym's double doors and walked up this aisle, accompanying a changing roster of student body leaders, a series of deans of
students and even three different college presidents.

Yet every year I worry that I might trip—on the steps that ascend to
the platform, over my carefully chosen words, or over an unexpected emotion that may lurch its way into my heart and surprise me. I am a college
chaplain. I work at a secular college, where few vestiges of our Presbyterian,
Christian heritage remain. In general Macalester, like many of its sister institutions, is a place in whose daily life God, or at least religion, doesn't play
an active role. One of the few remaining moments of institutional religious
expression is the tradition of the chaplain giving a prayer at formal events
like this. Today I am to usher another new class of students over the threshold to college. And I'll begin the ceremony with a prayer.

The student orientation leaders, upperclassmen, have created some
order to the line, by gathering the first-years in groups on the lawn, each
group clustered around a Scottish clan name with its tartan on a placard.
Students learn that Macalester's history is tied to Scotland, its founder a
Presbyterian Scot. Whether the students are from the United States or one

of ninety other nations represented in our student body, today they hover under these Scottish banners; today they are being initiated into the world of Macalester College: Scottish, American, Presbyterian, secular, international, multicultural, light-hearted, and intellectually rigorous.

As the procession begins, the bagpipes, now tuned, start wailing like newborn calves. The line of first-year students behind me streams down the long corridor outside the gym door and disappears around a corner. I am walking with the president, the dean of students, and the student government president. We make our way up the aisle behind the bagpipes (now accompanied by a drum), through a sea of empty folding chairs. Perched on the gym bleachers are the new students' parents, grandparents, siblings. As the bagpipers come up the aisle, the family members rise without prompting. Maybe they stand in honor of their child or in awe of this auspicious moment and all that has gone into getting here. Maybe they are thinking over the past twenty-four hours that have brought with them so much ferment: the last-minute packing at home, the long flight or longer drive, the stale hotel breakfast, the silence of their child as they together followed signs directing them to the unloading zone, where boxes, bags, laptops, and even the mini-refrigerator that sparked an argument a month ago about whether it was *really* necessary to bring, would soon be carted inside. What did they make of the guy in the tartan kilt directing parking? They must have known they weren't in Kansas anymore, or Scotland for that matter. Did they chuckle when they later discovered that he is the head of college security?

All over campus today, lumps rise in throats, tears spring to eyes, the small hand of a younger sister reaches for her older brother for what will be the last time in months. That little one is now standing by her parents on the bleachers, craning her neck to find her brother's face in the bobbing line of students. As the bagpipers continue their bleating, heartbeats race as students make their way down the aisle and find a seat on the metal folding chairs. Having made my way up the steps, I am now on the platform beneath the recessed basketball hoop. The bagpipers stand at attention in front of the platform, playing until the last student is seated. Then they make their way up the side aisles and back out the gym door. Their blast becomes a blare and then a muted bellow as they disappear down the hallway.

I am first on the program. I step to the podium. All eyes are on me. I drink in the moment, noting the remarkable diversity of students in front of me, feeling the stir of energy in this room full of eager young people, the undertow of banter among a few daring ones, disrupting the ceremony's formality. It is exciting. It is playful. It is time to start. I smile and spread my hands to include all the students, moms, dads, siblings, student leaders—even the college and student body presidents behind me. And then I speak as I would if I welcomed them as guests in my home: "Will you join me in prayer?"

But before I begin—before I call out to the "Holy Host of Life" or to the "Creative Spark of our Days," or any of the other names or images that help me remember that that even the most tender or troubling metaphor cannot fully capture who God is—I pause. I wait, holding the moment, because it is a moment that comes once a year, and for these students, once in a lifetime. By the end of this weekend, the young people in front of me will have left their family homes to become college students, their first step on the road to independent adulthood. As a parent whose own bright-faced daughter sat in one of these chairs not long ago, I pause to mark this moment of letting go. They are ready and they know the stakes are high.

I don't think I am the only one who brings awe and wonder to this moment, but attending to the emotional and spiritual life of the community is specifically what I am called to do. I am asked to notice the edges, the overlaps, the contradictions within the campus community. And I know I am certainly one of the best suited of the college personnel to do so. Because being a college chaplain at this time in history is nothing if not full of contradictions. I often feel out of place as a religious person in the secular academy. Often I wonder if the words I speak in public prayers or private conversations make any sense to a generation of postmodern young adults. I know what it is to have feet of clay as I lumber through my days.

Even in moments when my role should be clear—like now, offering an opening prayer—it can be riddled with ambiguity. How do these new students make sense of the fact that their official college experience begins with a chaplain-led prayer at a college that was presented to them in every glossy admissions brochure and website as an academically rigorous, *secular* institution? How do they reconcile my presence with Macalester's pride in its distinction as one of the top-ranked colleges in a national survey for "ignoring God on a regular basis"? For some, my presence and prayer may come as a great relief. For others, it may raise a concern. Some students and parents alike might worry the Admissions Office has misled them, that instead of the open-minded, cosmopolitan campus they chose, they've ended up in a little, midwestern, churchy place by mistake.

I, of course, know that what occurs on that stage, at that podium, is but one of many remarkably juicy juxtapositions that occur here, as at colleges everywhere. Students are asked to tackle the big questions of life's meaning and purpose, as they're simultaneously urged to take up a course of study that will lead to a productive and successful life. The young woman whose mother is undergoing chemo treatments and the young man recently diagnosed with bipolar disorder must also balance these life-jarring experiences with the expectations of faculty and institution to produce and perform with excellence. And jarring too: the debilitating homesickness that so surprises the student who deliberately chose to move as far as possible from the family he is already starting to miss.

Liberal arts educators take pride in plunging students into conflicting views with no absolutes. Students spend hours trying to make sense of material that may be obsolete a decade after they graduate. As their parents pay for tuition by refinancing the house, draining bank accounts, or amassing mortgage-sized loans, young adults know they are being launched into an economy where meaningful work is scant and that a good education is no longer a sure route to stability and prosperity. Macalester challenges them to expend hours serving others with an ideal of changing the world, but the institution sometimes has a harder time recognizing and honoring students' inner life of fear, worry, joyful wonder, and longing for love. But what liberal arts education has always known is that contradictions are critical to mobilizing action and, I would argue, to mobilizing faith. This generation faces daunting challenges as the globe warms and conflict among nations chills us, population explodes and the gulf widens between those who have and those who don't, as religious intolerance is on the rise and questions of the meaning and purpose of life itself awaken the need for ancient traditions to speak a fresh word to our world. Those of us who are in the role of educators realize our work is urgent. And, even on their first day as college students, these young people likely know it as well.

I often muse over the contested roles that define my work: Am I staff to the student crisis line? Or am I there for everyone in the community, to foster a safe space for each one to express his or her truth? Am I there to placate traditionalists by delivering "nice prayers" at nice occasions? Or am I there to prick the conscience of the campus on ethical and moral issues many would rather ignore? Are my questions to be political (what about the way the college invests its resources?) or more personal (why do we let loyal, long-term employees go without acknowledging their contributions)? Am I to support young people unconditionally as they make their way, mistakes and all? Or am I to challenge the "hook-up" culture that reduces sexual activity to recreation and often leaves lives littered with wreckage as a result?

I wonder if I am there as a professional whose specialization makes me ready to step in whenever a student's request sounds remotely religious. Am I there for all students, religious and anti-religious alike? Am I there to close the coffin on a faculty member, and to honor the impact of her life on the hundreds of students she taught? Or am I there to help quell anything that remotely reminds a sensitive student body of the fragility of life and keep the community firmly focused on bustling new beginnings?

As I reflect on the days and months and years that compose my working life, I quickly realize that my work is animated by all these many contradictions. That my job is to hold those contradictions as the very stuff of my own life and that of students, faculty, staff, and the entire academic community; to allow the power of the tension to energize, complicate, and awaken new insight that will allow us all, in turn, to serve others. The fact that I get to speak first at this convocation signals that I have a significant public role in the overall life of the college. But in truth, most of my work takes place out of view, behind the scenes, much of it in a chapel basement.

And my work is not all contradiction. There are clear expectations laid out by the institution. I am there to care for students, to pray for and with them—likewise for the faculty and the staff. For the young adults who have no way of guessing, as they sit at this convocation, that many of them will have a rough road ahead, I am there to assure them and their parents that I am a resource for support, guidance, or advice. It is into my hands that my institution has entrusted the care of young souls.

I am also there to shepherd a religiously diverse campus community. At Macalester our roots are nourished by our Presbyterian history but we have branched out in recent decades, providing a place for many religious, spiritual, cultural, and hybrid identities to nest. My work requires me to be highly literate in the range of traditions and practices in our midst and, simultaneously, to honor those who are firmly secular. My place at the center of these tensions feels especially vital in this post-9/11 world.

I am also there to call the community to prayer and reflection. When we mourn a beloved faculty member, or watch in helpless horror as a catastrophe replays over and over on the news, or, like now, are simply ushering in a new year at an opening ceremony, my role is to remind us that we live in times of deep anxiety and magnificent splendor. This is the closest most college chaplains come to being a priest, to standing in the midst of the community. Finding the words or holding the silence in those moments is my very humble contribution to helping Macalester navigate this highly charged and complex moment in history.

What one doesn't hear as I step to that podium the first day are these, more complicated dimensions of my work and the many questions that come my way in the course of a day or week: What does a chaplain *do* at a secular place like this? Are you the chaplain to the Muslim and Jewish students as well as to those who identify as Christian? Is your role to simply make the college look good to donors who might happen to be religious? No one else hears the words whispered to me at parent receptions or in late-night phone conversations: "Will you be there if my child has a panic attack, like he did this summer?" "Will you be there if her fragile faith comes unraveled by this terrible loss in our family?" And no one at all hears my own question: When that student finds her way to me, will I be adequate to the challenges she brings?

What those gathered at the convocation also don't *see* as they wait for me to begin the prayer is the whole series of life events, some magnificent and some terrifying, that have prepared me to be a chaplain of a college like this one. One sultry summer night when I was a young child, gazing up at the dazzling expanse of an Iowa sky, I felt the unmistakable presence of God. Today, my work with students who arrive in innocence, reaching for the stars in their own lives, takes me back to that night in my childhood, bringing wonder, joy, and awe.

In my journey as one of the first women ordained in the Presbyterian Church, I know the struggle and strain of young adults who counter the pressure to follow more conventional paths and instead take up their vocation of justice—racial, gender, environmental, economic.

And I know too the pain and shock that accompanies the first measure of trauma in a young life.

As a twenty-three-year-old seminarian, I was sexually assaulted by a stranger in the office of the church where I was a summer intern. When he left, I thought God and all my future plans walked out of there with him. But three years after the assault, I walked back into that same church to be ordained as a minister who would find her deepest joy in working with students as a chaplain.

My own journey toward healing and back to faith informs my every interaction with young people in need. This work is not only about the daily practice of drawing upon the deepest resources of faith, but about attending to the surprises of a life where God seems to show up where I least expect God to be.

Every year, at every convocation, I realize again that the young ones in front of me carry so much promise and so much pain in their tender hearts. There is something sacred going on even in the way they shift in their seats and so I take one last moment too—to be certain that I have my script, that the words I have prepared will slide freely from my lips, that I will honor this vocation of being a chaplain. I know that even in this prayer my work straddles the secular and sacred, the rational and irrational, the mind and heart. I pause because I am so honored to be there at that moment, as they take a gigantic step toward their heart's desires.

A fire burns at the heart of this day, Most Holy Fire of our lives.

Not a fire that consumes, O Creator, but a fire of passion, of hope,

purifying the hopes and dreams of those who gather in this place.

We give thanks for the gift of education, such an amazing privilege!

On this day, we especially celebrate the gifts of a new class of Macalester students,

a class with the promise of fiery spirits, brilliant minds and hearts.

Quicken the fire that burns in all our lives, this day, O fiery presence.

By the light of your countenance shine fiercely, boldly,

as a beacon for the world to see.

May ours be a torch of education

that lights the way for those who follow us.

AMEN

As I pour out the words of the prayer, I remind myself, mostly, that something, Someone, has been lighting our way for a long time. My prayer, if nothing else, is a reminder, a re-minder that a mind is a precious gift and must never be taken for granted. As I offer words of hope and gratitude, I am acutely aware of how they will sound to those gathered on this weekend fraught with excitement, worry, pride, and sadness. The reality is that I am the one at the convocation whose role it is to marshal these emotions. I find a catch in my own throat when I look up and see a tear rolling down the cheek of a young man in the second row, a mother on the aisle wiping her eyes. Everyone present brings to this place their greatest hope and their greatest fear, as only a new beginning can call forth. We are all standing at the threshold together; some will step over and others will turn back and return home. But in this moment, it's my job to ensure that none of us is alone.

CHAPTER 2

Opening the Door to the Chapel

January 2, 1994. Saint Paul, Minnesota

I STOOD, SHAKING, IN front of a locked chapel door. When I had left our new house that morning, the thermometer was registering twenty below zero. It was my first day on the job as the chaplain at Macalester College. It was January term, a time more for hibernation than heavy academic lifting. The campus was deserted, no one fool enough to venture out in such bitter climes, except me, I guess. It went through my mind, as I peered over the scarf wrapped around every possible inch of skin, that God had taken a powder on the place, and was down south with all the other snowbirds. But *I* was here. I was ready! "This is the new beginning You promised!" I thought, as much to reassure myself as to make any statement of faith.

My new boss, the dean of students, hadn't exactly told me where I should go when I arrived for my first day of work. I had not thought to ask. So when I came to the chapel building, where the chaplain's office was located, I paused. Which door to go in? I felt like a little girl arriving on the first day of school with my backpack stuffed with pencils, notebooks, and lunchbox but bewildered by which line of kids to join. Gingerly, I made my way down some snow-covered steps leading to the lower level chapel door. Holding a few books and a calendar, I steadied myself with the railing. *Why on earth had I chosen nice leather flats instead of boots?* Particles of ice hung in the air, uninterested in alighting on the frozen ground. My toes were numb, fingers tingling, and I cursed the wind as it twisted atop a snowdrift and sent a small avalanche toward me. I never knew snow could be sizzling but that morning it felt like bacon grease popping from a skillet onto my bare skin as I pulled my scarf down and exposed my eyes to search for the door handle. I tried it. Nothing happened. Frozen? I tried again. Not frozen . . . locked. Wrong door? I peered through the slim window. It was dark inside. No sign of life.

I am supposed to report for duty today and I'm locked out? How am I ever going to find the way in? I turned around to gaze across the campus, scanning for someone, anyone. But I was alone in the swirling snow.

Another mass of snow came plunging off the chapel roof, startling me. My eyes watered, my eyelashes frozen, my skin burning. Between my chattering teeth a prayer erupted: "Okay, God, you got me into this. Now, please, open the door!"

Of course I didn't expect God to rend the heavens and glide to my side with a golden key to abracadabra the door open. Though there had been enough moments in my life where I had been startled by a very immediate sense of God's presence, toppling grace, abundant mystery, this didn't turn out to be one of them. Standing at that door, my prayer arose more from the worry that had plagued me for months: that taking this job had been a huge mistake. That the locked door was a sign.

Another blast of ice-laden wind stung my cheek. Tugging on the firmly locked door one last time, I wondered again whether the job change that I had been interpreting for months as a call from God was actually a divine joke. But as I turned to leave, a young woman started down the steps towards me, pulling her mittens off to retrieve a key from a large tote. Unlike me, she was wearing huge boots, an even larger down coat, and a cozy-looking fake fur hat. She saw me at the door and with a friendly smile extended her un-mittened hand to me.

"Hi, I'm Kate. You must be the new chaplain. Who else would be out in this weather!"

Of all the greetings I have ever experienced this was one of the most welcome. Not only would she rescue me from the cold, but her energy and warmth immediately washed away my worries.

"I am so sorry I'm late. Our apartment building didn't get plowed out this morning and I couldn't reach you," she said as she moved to the door. "Oh, it is so bitter cold." And then, smiling, "Not a real *warm* welcome."

I thought Kate might be a student. As if she read my mind she said, "Oh, you probably wonder who I am. I am the chapel secretary. I came when Marvaleen left last fall. But anyway, let's get in out of the cold!" She opened the door and held it for me. We hurried inside.

As I stepped over the threshold leading into the chapel basement I suddenly thought, "There is no turning back." My second thought was surprise at my own apprehension. I had assumed I would be immediately enthralled as Macalester College's chaplain. But as I entered the lower level of the chapel and gazed around, a feeling of dread blanketed me. The space was barren and shabby. The walls were a bleak shade of gray and the dim lighting left me colder than I had felt a few moments earlier out in the drifting stir of Minnesota deep freeze. The stale air felt almost funereal. I quickly stomped these thoughts away along with the snow from my thin shoes.

When I had interviewed the previous spring, I had visited this space and seen where my office would be. It had not made much of an impression on me. I didn't remember that it had such a basement feel. A large pillar in the entryway interrupted my view of a sunken conversation pit: three steps down, with bench seating framing an open space. I also didn't remember the stained carpet or that the only thing covering the wall was a crookedly-hung movie screen that must have been closed up in haste months before and never reopened.

Kate flipped on the lights in the hallway. The fluorescent glow only made the scene look more forgotten and abandoned. I followed her down the hall. "Here's your office," she said, unlocking the door. She paused as she pointed towards the desk: "Dr. Meisel left some files for you. He was a nice man. Students liked him a lot. But I know they are ready for the permanent chaplain."

She turned and went back down the hallway, three empty grocery bags under her arm. "I have ordered your keys. I'll call to see if they're ready," Kate said over her shoulder. "Please let me know if I can get you anything else."

The door to my new office felt substantial as I pushed it open. It was heavy oak, not the cheap hollow doors used in so many offices I'd occupied. The handles were ornate, U-shaped, brass. It was clear that, despite its current shabbiness, the chapel building had been constructed with great attention to detail. Someone's artistry and excellent craftsmanship lay just beneath years of neglect. As I paused to admire the door, I already had an inkling that my work at this college would require being ready to hold that door open—to a hungry heart or worn soul, and to welcome the shimmering light of the holy. My mood began to lift. I thought about the "holy hospitality" I had promised in my interview. For that important work, not much was needed. I could hold the door open to deep questions, to brave ideas, to fear and vast insight. I knew that hospitality would be essential to awakening spirits, whether it be at a Saturday morning discussion group at my home or around a table in the chapel lounge with steamy soup and earnest conversations. I could already see it: the small love seat couch just inside the door would receive many students, faculty and staff members who would find their way to my office over the years. Thinking ahead to the joy of this work caused my pulse to quicken as I sat in my new office. *I have everything I need*, I thought. And for the second of many times that day, a wave of gratitude flooded over me.

My office was filled with boxes of books and desk supplies I had sent ahead from Wisconsin. I dug around in the desk and had just found a pair of scissors to begin opening the crates when I was stopped short by a tentative tap at the door. It was Kate.

"When you have a minute, I need to talk with you about something," she said.

"Oh, come on in, please," I said, smiling.

She made her way through the boxes to a chair.

"Well, I hate to do this to you, but I need to let you know I am resigning from this job. I took it in November thinking I'd be here a while but my husband is starting a doctoral program and we have to move to North Carolina so he can take a couple of classes this spring to prepare for the program next fall. Our families are there and we're excited. I'm sorry to tell you this just when you're starting. I don't know if Dr. Meisel told you, but I gave my notice a couple weeks ago." This detail must have gotten lost over the holiday break.

"No, I didn't know," I managed.

I must have looked totally stricken. I needed this person, badly. I hadn't a clue where the copy machine was, how to get voicemail or where to find a file folder, let alone the post office.

"Okay, wow," I finally said.

She dropped her glance, "Oh, and this is my last day."

There was nothing I could do about Kate's departure. And, after my first wash of panic, I was utterly sympathetic. I myself had just resigned from Carroll College. I knew well the cluster of feelings that arise when you look into the face of a person or community not ready to let you go: joy and excitement at the new; worry and fear about leaving; guilt after each small announcement when the eyes of the recipient well up or widen or turn aside.

College chaplains are accustomed to arrivals and departures. Of course most of the arrivals are new students. They show up on campus, spend several intensive years with us and then, as is the rhythm of our work, we send them on their way. Staff and faculty also come and go. A college campus is a proverbial revolving door. And though Kate's news was far from welcome, I simply said, "I'm excited for you." She looked at me with surprise and then said, "Thank you." Before she headed back to her office she said again, "If you need anything, let me know."

I turned toward the crates of books but instead decided to focus on the pile of file folders on my desk. Leafing through them, I realized that my predecessor, Dr. Donald Meisel, had left a treasure trove of files with correspondence between former chaplains and the chapel donor, a survey of student interests, and a list of the search committee members labeled, "For Future Reference." There was also a pile of unused gift certificates available for what he termed "nice job" rewards for students, some unopened mail and a welcome note from retired Macalester chaplain, Russ Wigfield, inviting my husband and me to dinner. I was overcome by this small gesture of kindness and was in the throes of another wave of gratitude when I heard a slam—the door of the chapel—followed by the stomping of heavy boots on the brick floor.

My mind immediately took a census of who was in the building, as it had reflexively done for years after that long-ago summer afternoon in Seattle, when I was assaulted. Since then, being alone in a building made me very anxious. But I wasn't alone—Kate was there. Before I had another thought, a young man appeared in the doorway. He was slight of build, wearing thick boots, a gray parka zipped up over his chin, a blue stocking cap and an orange and blue striped scarf. He unwound the scarf as if he were disrobing a mummy. And as soon as his mouth was revealed, he greeted me, extending a gloved hand.

"Chaplain Forster-Smith?"

"Yes," I said with a smile.

"I'm Nathan Steinberg. I wanted to be the first student to meet you. Did I accomplish my mission?"

I knew I would like this young man. He had twinkle, energy, and an appealing candor. But I had no way of guessing that the conversation we were about to have would shape my work at Macalester College in untold ways.

"Yes, as a matter of fact, you did," I said, chuckling. "Please come in. Sorry, not much space with all the boxes."

He looked around at the sealed cartons. "Wow, are these all full of your books?" he asked.

"Yes, how did you know? I love books. Sort of like friends that make their way over the miles with you." He laughed as he took off his gloves and hat.

I asked him where he grew up, what year he was at Macalester, and how he had been involved with the chapel program. "Well, I grew up in Boston. I am Jewish. Actually, that is one of the reasons I came by to see you. Chaplain Forster-Smith . . ."

"Oh, please call me Lucy," I leapt in. Nathan seemed a bit flustered by my casual engagement with him. I wondered if he expected a chaplain who was stuffier, formal, established. Or maybe that was my own worry.

"Okay, *Lucy*. Oh, that's weird . . ." he said, still flustered. (Over the next years he always called me "Chaplain.") "Anyway, L-L-Lucy, I have a question that I didn't raise with Dr. Meisel because I knew he was here for a short time. But it is something that I have concerns about. Being Jewish and knowing that Macalester has a lot of Jewish students, I am wondering: what do you think about taking the cross off the top of the chapel? A lot of us have talked about it and we find having it up there is really offensive. If it weren't there, the Jewish students might use the chapel at lot more."

Had I even noticed a cross on the chapel? No. And if I had noticed it, would I have thought it would be a problem?

I was dumbfounded. Whatever other surprises I'd been through that morning, I never expected to be confronted with a question as obviously charged and theologically loaded as this in my first two hours on the job. I stared at him for what was quickly becoming an awkward length of time. I had the clear sense that there was a test in his question. It was my first taste of the fact that all bets on what was known as "Minnesota nice" were off in this little collegiate island of questing, questioning, challenging, and deeply healthy probing. In time, it would come to be one of my favorite attributes of Macalester students. But today, the intensity and the high stakes of Nathan's abrupt question completely threw me.

Dumb*founded*. My temptation was to go to the foundings, dig around in the university archives, to take Nathan on a long campus tour telling him everything I had just read in a book sent to me by Dr. Meisel about the College's founder, the Rev. Edward Duffield Neill. Rev. Neill was frontier pastor who started Macalester in 1874, a time when Minnesota was a gateway to the West, and most of the country's educated citizenry was still "back East." Presbyterian leaders like Neill thought it quite *reasonable* in all senses of that word to take bright young men and give them a deeper understanding of the world in the late nineteenth century.

I suspected that the other chaplains of this college whom I had read about would never have faced anything like the kind of question Nathan had posed to me that morning. Fifty or sixty years earlier, Macalester's first chaplain, Maxwell Adams, would never have dreamed of squaring off with a student over the presence of a cross on the chapel. Those were the days when Protestant Christian chaplains had a clear and significant role on college and university campuses. Dr. Adams taught in the religion department, presided at the college's required (Protestant) chapel services, married and buried members of the community, held forth with moral guidance in public settings, and was frequently summoned to the president's office as an advisor. Dr. Adams was a global citizen, unapologetically rooted in mainline Protestant Presbyterianism. Students under his watch may have been Lutheran, Quaker, Roman Catholic, and Jewish, but they were quite aware that Macalester College was Presbyterian, a college of the church. If they had concerns about the required chapel program and the courses in Bible, they kept those to themselves.

I suspect that, as Alvin Currier took the reins as chaplain from Dr. Adams in the 1960s, Al too never paused to wonder about a cross being placed prominently on the chapel. There were too many storms raging through the hallowed halls of campuses like Macalester with the civil rights movement leading into Vietnam War protests, a newly legislated drinking age of eighteen, the new availability of the birth control pill and its attendant sexual freedom, and young people's growing suspicion of all institutionally held power. Chaplains on many liberal campuses including Macalester College may have shed the churchy affects of the 1950s but there was still no escaping the fact that their role was an institutionally freighted one. Their social justice commitments and liberal theological positioning put them squarely in the eye of many political storms. Many chaplains, responding to and supporting the youth movements on their campuses, challenged their ordaining bodies to find ways to engage in the widespread social upheaval underway. After all, the chaplains were living in the midst of that upheaval—they could not ignore it.

Throughout the 1970s, 80s, and 90s chaplains found ourselves confronted with institutions that were coming unmoored from their religious
foundings. Many colleges and universities redirected their religious life
program funds into counseling centers, student life programs, and offices
for multicultural life, assuming that the functions traditionally assigned to
the chaplain would be taken up, albeit piecemeal, in other settings. The
scrutiny of institutions that was so prominent in the 1960s didn't go away
during these decades and with the rise of the Moral Majority and Christian
Right, it was difficult for those of us who are Christian but not allied with
these groups to be very convincing. The shouting of these voices was too
loud and the liberal Protestant voice that held sway in the 1930s through
the early 1960s went quiet. There was the carry-over of social justice commitments. Women were being ordained in many quarters of the church.
The AIDS crisis brought liberal Christian voices out of their silence in response to the vitriolic pronouncements of our fellow Christians that AIDS
was God's judgment on gay people. The Iraq War in the 1990s, followed
by 9/11, awakened a generation of young people to the need for interfaith
engagement, multifaith awareness and leaders, pastors, priests, chaplains,
rabbis, imams, who would unapologetically stand in their religious or spiritual traditions and hold the way open for deep engagement with difference.

But that day, with Nathan in front of me, I left this history lesson in
the dusty recesses. Instead, I looked into the eyes of this bright, motivated,
amazing young man and decided to ask him to help me understand.

"So, Nathan, tell me about how students see that cross. What does it
mean to them?" As it turned out, this opened the way to a remarkable conversation about religious life at Macalester, about marginal voices and nor-
mative ones, about, yes, the history of the college. Nathan felt strongly that
Jewish students need to have barriers like the cross removed since crosses
had been used against Jews and Muslims and even Christians many times
over too many centuries. I noticed that as he talked, Nathan was smiling,
nodding and leaning forward in the chair, rather than his earlier drawn-
back posture. Perhaps we were getting somewhere. Then he caught my eye
and held it. He paused and asked his question again.

"So, what do you think of taking the cross off the top of the chapel,
Chaplain . . . Lucy?"

There was still a little heat in the question, arising from what I now
saw was his own non-negotiable passion. He meant no disrespect. But he
was asking me to come clean with my thinking so I had no choice.

"Nathan, you've asked a huge question and one that I know we have to deal with here at Macalester. I honestly don't know the exact history of why there is a cross on this building. I can guess it is there to remind all who see it of the College's Presbyterian Christian history." Nathan was looking down, fussing with the fringe on his scarf. I went on, "I don't know about you, but I am convinced that there is a lot of pull in our society to forget our history, forget where we came from. This is true especially with religion. There are a lot of people who assume that religion is something we should ignore and hope it will go away. But I think it is really important to pay attention to how much influence it has and to recognize how religiously committed people have contributed positively to society. I guess one of those ways was starting colleges like Macalester."

He had lifted his eyes from the scarf and now they were fixed on my face. He shifted in the chair. I noted he still had his jacket on and wondered if he was about to bolt out the door.

"So, what do you think?" I asked.

"Well, I'm not convinced of what you are saying but I do see your point about history. I guess if this were Brandeis University I wouldn't expect the Jewish symbols to come down. But I still think we should talk more about it," he said.

I sensed that the cross was only the starting point of the conversation. I ventured in a slightly different direction.

"Nathan, I see my work here to support all the students, no matter what their religious tradition. I want to make sure that by the time you leave Macalester you have the best experience you can as a Jew. I'd like to talk more about the cross. I need more background on how it got there. I'm not even sure if I am in a position to take it down. But you've given me a lot to think about."

I remember this conversation like it was yesterday. From the vantage point of many years later, it all sounds so smooth. I know there were moments when I halted, reached for words that were not coming, saw Nathan look out the window, or adjust his fogged-over glasses, fidgeting. I had given my best response but there was something in the exchange that left us both unsatisfied. As he finally pulled on his hat and headed out the door, I wondered if I would ever see him again.

Nathan's visit haunted me for many days and weeks following our exchange. It wasn't the politics of his question that bothered me, it was his urgency. He had sought out his chaplain with a question of real significance for his young life. What I couldn't forget was the look in his eye, the slight quiver at the corner of his lip, the bravado that held its ground but also in some odd way, gave ground to meet upon. Thinking of him in the doorway that morning, my very first visitor, I remembered my own troubled face at age twenty, entering the office of my seminary chaplain. I knew what it was like to carry high-stakes questions into a chaplain's office. And though the situation that prompted my questions many years before was very different from our exchange that day, I saw in Nathan's face the same force that mine had held.

Through the first months of my time at Macalester College I came to realize that my job as chaplain was to look into faces: of those arriving at my door, or sitting across the table in the cafeteria, hurrying past on slippery sidewalks. That my work was to notice when the slight tip of a student's head might indicate heavy regrets or the averted eyes of a faculty member might be a subtle invitation for a gentle "How are you?" To be ready when the door opens suddenly and I see in a student's face the dark under-eye circles that a hint of a long night, but also the energy of some new miracle about to burst through. Nathan's visit helped me realize with clarity I have never forgotten that in all of these moments, my work is to cross the threshold of the heart.

CHAPTER 3

Being Called

"The Lord called Samuel again, a third time.
And he got up and went [to] Eli and said, 'Here I am, for you called me.'
Therefore Eli said to Samuel, 'Go, lie down; and if he calls you,
you shall say, 'Speak, Lord, for your servant is listening.'"

1 Samuel 3:8–9

PROBABLY AT NO OTHER time in life is the vocational question, that is, the question *what shall I do with my life?*, more pressing than during the college years. Most students assume that college will prepare them to take up work that will provide an economic edge over their non college-educated peers. They may not know the exact profession that will follow from an education at a place like Macalester College. But their focus is not only on what will pay the bills (including the unsubsidized loans that are amassing interest as they move through the four years), but on finding meaningful work, work that contributes and makes a difference in the lives of others and in the world. The closer they get to the end of their college experience, the more urgent the questions become: How do they know what kind of work they are equipped for? And who will assure them that they are doing what they are "meant" to do?

"How do I know it's God calling me?" Johanna asked at a retreat focused on vocation the Macalester chaplain's office hosted one fall evening. "How do I know it isn't just my grandma's voice in my head? She wanted me to be a doctor, you know. I want to be a doctor. I want to work in parts of the world that don't have access to healthcare. Is that God? Is that my grandma? Does it matter?" At the same retreat, Jim asked: "Do I trust my heart, my head, or my professors?" Though not everyone would frame the questions in this way, students like Jim and Johanna have a sense that they were placed on this planet to do a particular work. They resonate with the oft-quoted Frederick Buechner definition of the word: "[Vocation] means the work a man [sic] is called to by God. . . . The place God calls you to is the place where your deep gladness and the world's deep hunger meet."[1] For Jim and Johanna, the responsibility of discovering and identifying this meeting place between gladness and hunger is a real preoccupation.

It doesn't take long, when I am in conversations with students about their life direction for them to ask me how I got into my own line of work. It surprises me how hungry they are to hear my personal reflections on my own life's calling.

I admit that I have mused for years over this same question. It has been challenging to locate an exact moment when I knew I was called to be a college chaplain. But it is equally challenging to identify the moment when I felt the urge to become a parent or to marry my life partner, or to pursue seminary. What constitutes a true moment of calling? And where does it come from? Is it God or is it the world? Is it my ego or an instinctual response to someone in need? Is it a friend, a mentor, or something else altogether? Is the only valid call one that comes as a voice in the night, like the one the boy Samuel heard when he was in the house of the priest, Eli? I've never had that experience. My experience of call is more like an accumulated stack of the pink "while you were out" phone message slips that used to clutter my work mailbox. As I reach for one, many others tumble out.

When I tell my vocational narrative to students, I share a story of my first profound experience of God, as I sat on the house steps with my father one summer night when I was four. But I also tell a far more complicated story, the story of my interview and subsequent call to Macalester College, the place they know well. My story dispels a lot of assumptions students and others may have that ministers have an inside track on the "call" thing. Indeed it is true that some people, like the Hebrew prophets of old, describe the call of God as a blast in the night. It is also true that others, religious and

---

1. Buechner, *Wishful Thinking*, 95.

otherwise, experience the pleasure of an affirmation in the smiling faces of an admiring search committee. I experienced neither of these.

My "call" to Macalester College began, metaphorically enough, with a ringing phone. On a February morning in 1993, about a year before I arrived at the locked chapel at Macalester, I was sitting in my office at Carroll College in Waukesha, Wisconsin, where I had been chaplain for almost four years. When I picked up the phone, my friend Scott, one of the chaplains at Columbia University, was on the other end. Anytime I hear a familiar voice on the phone with no context or warning, I am wont to assume it is trouble—someone has died; someone is being fired; someone is being accused of something awful and needs counsel. Or I think the person on the other end needs something from me—perspective on a problem or a fill-in speaker for a last-minute cancellation. Scott was a one of my seminary buddies, and through the years following seminary we always connected at chaplaincy gatherings, over a glass of something.

After a bit of small talk, Scott launched into his agenda.

"Lucy, I have a job opportunity for you to consider. Macalester College is looking for a chaplain and I think you'd be great for it."

My heart jumped and sank at the same time. Scott was single; Scott could bolt off to a job like that in a flash. I was married with three kids, a cat, a bird, and a settled life. Feeling myself tied to so many other lives was the sinking part. The jumping part, the heart that hit my throat within seconds of his encouragement, was the thrill of a new opportunity arriving out of the blue to put a new destination on the map. Macalester College. I knew the place. I had gone up from Wisconsin to Macalester in Minnesota a couple of years earlier to consult with the very talented young professional who had started their community service program. I knew it was an excellent college, Presbyterian-affiliated, progressive.

"Wow, it sounds great. But Scott, why not you? Why aren't you going for it?"

"Oh, I'm not looking to move right now. Things are good here. But I know Macalester's dean of students, Ed DeCarbo. He and I worked together here at Columbia. When I heard about the job I immediately thought of you. I think you and Ed would be very simpatico."

We chatted a bit more and I hung up the phone, promptly forgetting about his suggestion. Moving to Minnesota was so clearly impossible; it didn't merit further thought.

A few days later I collected the mail from my mailbox and a letter fell out from among the periodicals and brown campus-mail envelopes. It was hand-addressed to me from the guy who headed up the Presbyterian Church's higher education office. Too curious to wait, I opened the envelope as I made my way across the icy February sidewalks from the post office. The envelope contained a position description for the Macalester chaplain job, along with a note from Clyde, the higher education executive. The note simply said, "Think about this job. It reads, 'Lucy.'" My heart jumped back to my throat.

When I got back to my office I looked over the position description and indeed, I knew I had experience in everything it outlined. I had to admit—it *did* read "Lucy." But the kids, Tom, selling the house . . . I was getting way ahead of myself. Besides, they wouldn't hire me. They'd be looking for someone more famous, like the chaplain who had just vacated the position—Coffin was his name, the nephew of the famous William Sloane Coffin of Yale University, who was probably the most famous college chaplain in history. I didn't toss the job description but I didn't bring it up at home either.

Things were rough at Carroll College leading up to that February. Due to budget cuts, faculty and staff as well as whole departments were falling under the knife. My job had been downsized though I wasn't let go. I watched as my own boss was escorted out of his office. It was simply depressing. But I had determined to stay at Carroll, figuring I'd weathered the storms up to then, so surely smooth sailing was ahead. It was just as I was figuring out what I needed to do to rebuild in the wake of devastation that these two contacts about the position at Macalester appeared. I tried to be open to my trusted and supportive colleagues Scott and Clyde, to listen to their words and accept their encouragement, but I still needed to withhold any emotional engagement with them because of the obvious facts: I simply could not leave.

On the other hand, our family's financial needs were growing as our children moved from toddlers to school age. Tom and I spent many nights worried about making ends meet. He had a good position at an urban Presbyterian church but given the reality of three growing children, it didn't cover the salary decrease that had been leveled at me during the budget cuts. I also was feeling uncertain about my long-term role at the college—and about whether the college would even survive this massive wave of changes.

When yet another phone call came a day later, this time from another colleague who claimed she didn't know that Clyde and Scott had been in touch, I couldn't brush it off any longer. Three messages are hard to ignore. I broached the subject of the Macalester position with Tom, and to my great amazement he encouraged me to apply. I was confused by his response. We had already moved once for the Carroll job and I assumed he'd be reluctant to undertake another round of my career disrupting his. In addition, our children were thriving in this very cozy college town, with ample babysitters, great schools, and tons of friends up and down the block. Though I didn't fully understand the basis for Tom's encouragement, I went ahead, submitting my dossier, the required cover letter, and asking non-Carroll people to serve as references so I wouldn't signal ambivalence about my current job. I waited.

What I wanted was a voice, a clear signal, something that would assure me that taking this new position was my best next step. *How do I know it's God calling me?* Rather than a voice, after I mailed my application I received a long silence. I had thought they were looking to fill the position by summer but it was almost April and I had received no word.

On a Friday afternoon, just as the snow was starting to melt, I opened my mailbox to find a thin envelope from Macalester. It was a rejection letter. I was very disappointed but also relieved. I had been wondering all along about whether or not the job would be right for me and my family and even if the answer had come back "no," it came as a relief to have at last received a clear signal.

That was, until Monday morning. I had an early meeting and when I checked my office inbox, I found a pink phone message note asking me to call Macalester's Human Relations Office. I dialed the number, already wondering what other, more successful, applicant had offered my name as a reference.

"Reverend Forster-Smith?"

"Yes."

The friendly woman from Human Resources spoke with a flat Minnesota accent. "We have had a change in our process and are very embarrassed that you may have received a letter from us about your employment status."

"Yes, I did receive the letter on Friday."

"Well, we sent the letter to you by mistake and would like to invite you to stay on our short list of candidates for the chaplain position."

I sat for a moment unable to respond. Sophisticated places like Macalester College don't send rejection letters by mistake. This was highly unusual. I finally found the words. "Sure, I would be happy to stay in your pool." The satisfaction of my "clear signal" had vanished, but in its place I was surprised to find a new ember of hope.

Whenever I am at a major turning point in my life or when I receive the inkling that something big is coming my way, I get the same feeling in the pit of my gut as I did as a child in Iowa when a storm was brewing. Our storms usually came out of the west. They would often come on sultry summer afternoons, often just as we were headed to the local swimming pool for relief. The sky would turn a sallow yellow, almost jaundiced. I would hear distant thunder rolling and rippling over the vast plains out past Omaha. The wind would rustle a few leaves as the yellow sky turned ebony. Everything would go still. It was as if the very earth herself held her breath. And then, almost as quickly as the envelope of silence had arrived, it was broken by a sudden clap of thunder and jabbing lightning. The streetlights would jolt on just as the pelting would begin.

I still expect momentous change to come into my life with this same thundering presence, to start out on the horizon and then make its way overhead in a form impossible to ignore. At times, it does. But other times, momentous change comes much more slowly, with no signals of warning.

Whenever I wonder about how I am to distinguish the voice of God in moments of confusion, I am reminded of my earliest experience of God when I was a young child. It was not a voice from the outside, but something almost as clear—a thought and erupting light that set me on a journey I have continued for the rest of my life.

It was on a hot Iowa night a few weeks after my fourth birthday. That night my dad and I had done what we must have done most sticky July nights that summer. With the house unbearably hot, we escaped to the front steps. The night's uneasy quiet foretold a thunderstorm that would likely arise out of the west and bend the cottonwood tree at the foot of our sloping lawn. Sometimes that tree doubled over like a back bent in scrubbing. But that night, the tree was eerily still.

The stars held us rapt as we sat there, gazing upward. Millions of them. A packed sky, some winking, some glaring, some light-years faint. But that sky, with stars shimmering, holding our gaze, gave way to a sky set ablaze. It grew bright, swirling before my big brown eyes.

"Daddy," I said reaching for his thick arm, "look at the stars."

"Yes," he replied. Silence.

"Daddy, they are really bright . . . see?" *Did he see them? Really see them?* Silence.

And then, as the stars burned before my eyes, a thought came to me: "How can anyone not know there is a God?"

Did I hear God speaking to me? Not exactly. Did I identify this as a mystical experience at the time? Heavens no. But in that moment, out on the cement steps, up on a hilly bluff, with a night so humid and close that only the mosquitoes were able to muster any energy to move, something deep within my little four-year-old frame burned with a fire that has not been quenched since.

"Daddy, look," I said again. Silence.

"Sweetie, it is getting late. Let's go in before we get carried away by these five-pound mosquitoes," he said.

Even now, more than a half-century later, I am not sure what happened that night. Was I so enthralled with the sky and the stars that I blurred my eyes, or was it a comet that made its way across the sky and I caught the tail of it in my view? Or perhaps it *was* something of a miracle, a sky awakened by the mystery of a Creator who allowed my ready eyes to see what adults so often miss—what children may see but then tuck away into the thick undergrowth of childhood. I don't recall telling my parents what happened, even my dad who was with me. I do recall that the rest of that night I lay in my bed, very awake.

I don't think of myself as particularly spiritually precocious. I know people who are. There are people who bring to their relationships or to the classroom a depth of spiritual insight and perspective that stuns others. They drop pearls of wisdom about the most mundane things, drawing upon some inner stream of knowledge that eludes me. But I do think that having a very early experience of seeing something magnificent beyond my comprehension, realizing a connection with the Great Unseen, and holding what I thought was a great secret because the adult next to me had seemed not to notice this profound moment unfolding, has set me on a life's course in some very specific ways.

First, because I was so young when this happened, I didn't interrogate its authenticity. It happened and I accepted it. It was true just like any other element of my daily life was true. I was so very excited about what I was seeing. I knew my father was a very religious man. He was a leader in our Baptist church. I learned later that when he was in college he had thought of going into the ministry. He decided to take other paths. As I tried to share what had happened, my dad didn't respond. He clearly didn't see it, or if he did, he didn't let on that he had. I realized that I was alone in this experience of intense mystery.

The sudden shift from being rejected to being asked to stay in the pool of candidates wasn't exactly the sky lighting up but certainly sent an emotional bolt into the steady pace of life in small-town Wisconsin.

A few weeks after I received the second-chance phone call, I was invited to an in-person interview at Macalester. I flew from Wisconsin to St. Paul, Minnesota on a bright May morning. Upon arriving, I discovered that the man who would be my boss, Ed DeCarbo, was away from campus with a very ill parent. The kind secretary assured me that though it was a busy time of year, they had scheduled a number of sessions for students, faculty and staff to meet the chaplain candidate—I would definitely meet lots of members of the community. She was right and wrong. A number of people did show up, but the combination of finals week and the gorgeous weather meant a few scheduled sessions with no takers at all. When I found myself sitting in a room with a folding table, folding chairs, ripped carpeting and a soiled couch alone for twenty-five minutes, I decided that I didn't want to miss the beautiful day either. I left a note for any latecomers and made my way outside.

I found an available chair at the edge of a sunny patio, feeling out of place in my fancy interview clothes, but struck by the fact that no one even noticed me. I attempted to catch the eye of someone who might be open to a question or two about Macalester College but spring fever was high and finals week was pulsing, so I set aside my agenda and simply observed the scene.

Students basked on the lawn and in chairs strewn across the patio. A group of students, all with waist-length hair, sat on cushions that matched the furniture I had seen in the Campus Center building. One of the students, androgynous, had a guitar in hand, and strummed rapidly as the others smoked cigarettes and smiled. A series of long tables ran down one end of the patio with students collecting signatures on petitions for various causes. Most of the crowd was lounging on blankets under a canopy of cherry blossoms.

I was struck by how different this scene was from Carroll College. Students at my college were by-the-book-types. They wore sweats, Carroll t-shirts, backward baseball caps, and the most progressive types expressed their "edge" through their academic life and community service work. Not much on the shirtsleeve, as they'd say. The students before me at Macalester had more skin exposed, for one thing. Lots of guys with shirts off, ripped jeans, bare feet. Some of the women wore halter-tops, jeans that skimmed their belly buttons, or very short cut-offs. There was the juggler, who had bowling pins swirling overhead. And there was the group clustered around a bearded man, who seemed to be giving an academic lecture on the lawn, judging by the pace of his comments and the number of times his hands moved through the air. Students were rapt at whatever he was saying. I was rapt observing their level of attention on a day that would have had me with a serious case of spring fever.

After about twenty minutes, I glanced at my watch and realized that my meeting with the chaplain search committee was about to start. I stopped at a snack bar for a fortifying can of Coke and then climbed the steps to a quiet conference room to await the committee.

The first person to arrive was a student, Risa. She was very friendly, with a fresh smile, dark hair and brown eyes. I found out she was involved with the Christian Fellowship on campus. She quickly told me she was graduating and was moving to the East Coast.

"I wanted to be on this committee," she told me, "because Macalester needs God."

Before I had a chance to respond or wonder how many others shared her opinion, our conversation was interrupted by others filing in. They were cordial, casually dressed, smiling, welcoming. They took their places at the table. An older woman quipped, "We always seem to sit in the same places for these interviews." Most chuckled and a student said, "Yeah, you'd think we'd be always changing it up, this being Macalester." A wasp that had been dancing across the neon light fixture chose this moment to swoop low, causing a couple of us to duck. "Damn wasps," a distinguished-looking older man said. All eyes turned to me for a response. I shrugged and smiled. Ice broken . . . sort of.

As I sat at the end of the table, perched on the edge of a folding chair, the first question came at me from the faculty member who had introduced himself as convener for the day (not chairperson, "convener"): "So, why Mac?" He looked at me, expressionless. I glanced around the long table at the professors, students, and professional staff. There were about ten in all, some reclining in their chairs with arms crossed, others scanning what was likely my dossier, and a few leaning forward, their faces turned to me. Though the convener projected a level of enthusiasm that fell some place between tired and bored, the rest of the group was peppy. I was pleasantly surprised at their energy, especially when they could have been out enjoying the beautiful day instead of indoors under fluorescent lights. I struggled to sound lively even as I gave what I could tell was a generic response to the question.

"I have known of Macalester College for years with its connection with the Presbyterian Church and I came over from Carroll College a couple years ago to consult with your Community Service people about your amazing program of outreach and service. I'm ready for a change from where I've been. I think it would be exciting to join you in shaping a chaplaincy that moves toward the twenty-first century." A few people nodded. I began to relax.

A second question came from a staff member who introduced herself, a little mysteriously, as being from a "prominent office on campus." "What is your vision for this position?" she said. This time my words flowed, competent, confident. "Holy hospitality, that's what my vision for chaplaincy is about," I said. "Holding the door open, inviting others to cross the religious threshold that awaits them, even in the late twentieth century, when religion is suspect by many. Especially during the college years when the spiritual may get pushed to the edges, what I mean by holy hospitality is a way of holding the door of the heart open."

My few minutes in the gorgeous hum of the May afternoon had filled me with inspiration, the same kind of inspiration I was now promising to deliver to students through the programs I'd offer. I was in the middle of describing an alternative spring break trip to Appalachia when I noticed a bearded faculty member whose eyes had glazed over with boredom. My newfound confidence wavered. I heard myself say, "Students at Carroll were looking for ways to demonstrate their faith through action." When I glanced at the bearded professor again, he was looking right at me.

"Few people here are that into religion, so don't get your hopes up that many will be interested in what you have to offer," he warned.

I sat quietly and managed to nod, but my heart pounded blood into my cheeks. Was this the sentiment of the entire committee? If so, why were they even looking for a chaplain? Had this whole day been a waste? But just as these thoughts started racing through my mind, I noticed a restless stir making its way around the room. Another faculty member glanced at a third one, who was discreetly rolling her eyes. I wasn't sure if the roll was aimed at me or at the cynical faculty member. A staff member at the end of the table leaned back.

The buoyancy I'd experienced earlier was deflating quickly. I tried to figure out if it was just the weary spirits of a spent search committee, disappointment with my answers, or annoyance with this particular faculty member who the others may have found a little too forthright. For what seemed like a long time, we sat in silence, the bearded professor looking a little smug—perhaps pleased to have successfully burst my optimistic bubble. I was just starting to worry that everyone was waiting for me to say something when someone else broke the silence.

"I have a question." We all turned towards the young woman with a furrowed brow and abundant curls barely contained by a bandana. I had noticed this student taking copious notes while I was talking earlier. Now, her pen trembled in her hand. She caught my eye, held it with her pooling blue ones, and spoke. "There is a lot of trouble in the world," she ventured, "and in my experience it is often religion that creates the problems. I want to make the world a better place and lots of my friends, religious or not religious, do also. If you are our chaplain, how will you help us get ready for life after Macalester?"

All the students at the table and a few others nodded. So they didn't all agree with the bearded professor. Some of these folks really understood the possibilities of my role. The student who had asked the question, Clare, sat with her eyes fixed on me, waiting. I thought I could see what she hoped for in me: a spiritual leader who would go the distance, care for students' souls and challenge them to love the world, be supportive of their dreams and give them lots of practice in cultivating their skill in being agents of global change. I relaxed, smiled, and dove into answering her question.

I left the interview and flew back to Carroll College for its graduation ceremonies the next day. Admittedly, I was intrigued by Macalester. The odd and unsettling interview had left me worried that if I were offered the job and decided to do it, programming would not be my only challenge—if the weary and somewhat cynical members of the search committee were any indication, I would also have to convince people that a chaplain was a legitimate and needed role in the life of the campus. And I still hadn't met the man who was to be my boss.

But it was not only these external factors that left me unsettled. Unlike other job searches I had conducted in the past, this one had none of the "markers" I had come to trust, as signals that a change was needed: funding shuts down or a decent supervisor becomes an ogre or the new setting promises friendships as well as good work. I had to remind myself that in all of my past job searches the stakes had been lower, at least in terms of family needs. Tom's first job out of seminary, as an assistant minister, had landed him in Ohio. I followed him to Ohio and eventually found a position at a small college, we got engaged and married. We commuted between towns 165 miles apart. The second call came with a badly-needed phone call after Tom had left an unhappy job situation without another placement lined up. The third, to Carroll, had brought me into chaplaincy and Tom into a great parish situation. Our children had still, literally, been portable. Wisconsin had promised great friendships, the joys of living in a small town, and a welcome, driving-distance proximity to my family in Iowa.

The Macalester interview shot holes in all my assumptions about the content of a calling. As encouraging as it had been in some ways, it had put to rest none of my fears about whether or not relocating to Minnesota was the right move for me and my family. The worry kept nagging at me: if this opportunity was a call from God, shouldn't that be obvious?

The story of God's call to the people in Genesis chapter 12 comes first and foremost as a disruptive word. It is a word that requires the hearer to surrender control, to leave behind the treasures of his life and to place trust in the unseen—a crazy thing to do, but so compelling that there is no turning back. "Go" is the word that is spoken. "Go from your country and your kindred and your father's house to the land that I will show you." Abram's question may have been, "Why me, why now?" But his question also may have been, "How can I do anything else?" It is Yahweh calling, after all! And I have a feeling that whatever doubts Abram may have had about whether he was doing the right thing, when the tent stakes were pulled up and the entire tribe was on its way, the word "Go" rang in his ear.

But what if God doesn't speak quite so clearly to you? What if you've never been bowled over by a voice? What if the little tug inside you leaves you wondering if it was just your digestive tract, or a small measure of boredom, or a little guilt thrown on you after years of ease and contentment? How do you know if you are doing what is most true, most needful, most right, given all the possibilities and all the damn distractions? Or as Johanna asked at the vocation retreat, "How do I know it is God?" I continuously ask the same question.

That night on the porch when I was four had another outcome for me. Not only did it invite me to make a connection between the splendor of the world and my own sense of wonder, but that night also gave me a thirst to know the Source of the stars, of the erupting sky and of the reaching feeling it provoked in me. It set in motion a relationship with God, a close intimate relationship with the One who flung stars like pebbles tossed by a child. I wanted to talk with God, to listen to God. That night planted in me a lifetime's longing to find a way back to that feeling I experienced beneath the stars, but also a desire to take my seat with others who had also looked into the face of the night and felt the light of the universe break into the darkness. When I encounter students who are earnestly searching for a connection to the divine and a way to answer a call in their own lives, I recognize that desire immediately.

After the Macalester interview, the sky didn't light up and I certainly didn't hear a voice from above imploring me to "Go." At first, the phone didn't even ring. I figured the second thin envelope would soon be in the mail.

But the letter didn't come and a few days later, the phone did ring. This time it was the dean of students, the future boss who'd been out of town during my visit. He invited me to return for another interview. I assumed I was one among several finalists.

When I arrived back on campus things were very quiet. It was now summer and only a very few students lounged on the green lawn. I made my way back to the same office I'd entered two weeks before. This time, Dean DeCarbo's door was open. I reintroduced myself to the nice secretary. "Oh, yes, I remember you. How could I forget the pink jacket you wore to your interview?" *Was this a good sign or a bad one?* I tried to push the question out of my mind. But when I walked into his office, the dean's extended hand and kind smile allayed my worry. Dressed to the nines with a sea-blue tie that picked up the turquoise threads in his elegant tweed jacket, a tiepin, slacks, and polished shoes, he oozed class. Though more formal than I was used to, he was also hospitable. We walked down the block to a little restaurant. Over lunch he asked me some questions about my vision for the position, my experience and, in turn, was very forthright about the challenges and opportunities at the place even I was beginning to refer to as "Mac." What began as a serious discussion gave way to some laughter, and I caught a glimmer in his eye that made me hope this might just work.

He paid the bill and as we walked back to his office, a few yards from the chapel door that I would later, memorably, encounter locked, he offered me the job. I was stunned at how quickly he had decided to hire me. I thought he would let me go home and would call me if it was a "go." Not so. I learned later that when Ed decided on something, he acted.

As I boarded the airplane heading back home, I thought of Frederick Buechner's reflections on his own calling. Remembering an exchange with another guest at a formal dinner, he wrote: "'I hear you are entering the ministry,' the woman said down the long table, meaning no real harm. 'Was this your own idea or were you poorly advised?'"[2]

There have been times in my life when I have wondered if I was poorly advised. But looking out the window of the plane as I headed home, my soul quaking with the excitement and terror of new possibility, I was closer to Buechner's imagined response to the woman questioning his vocation: "[T]he answer that she could not have heard even if I had given it was that it was not an idea at all, neither my own nor anyone else's. It was a lump in the throat. It was an itching in the feet. It was a stirring in the blood at the sound of rain."[3]

Indeed, indeed. I knew that lump, I knew the itch, and I felt a stir in my blood. That evening on the plane, I realized that to be called is a combination of listening to one's heart, paying attention to what breaks it or lightens it, and recognizing moments when gifts, ideals, aspirations, and care awaken. It is complicated. It is challenging enough to know when an opportunity is the right one, or the best one, or the most professionally and personally advantageous, let alone to determine with any surety whether it is a call from God. It becomes even more complicated when you are asked to navigate the multiple callings that arise out of a day's work or a chorus of voices.

In this instance the most important voices in my life greeted me at the gate in Milwaukee. Tom and our three children caught my eye, and ran to me with swooping squeals of love. Though I was happy and excited to have the job offer in hand, I knew the tough part was ahead: breaking the news to Tom. He had been holding down the fort as I went through the interview process while also facing the reality that the "good news" might mean we'd have to move. I wanted to give us both time to think, so I delayed

2. Buechner, *Alphabet of Grace*, 109.

3. Ibid., 109–10.

my response to Macalester's offer until Tom had the chance to explore with the Presbyterian executive about job possibilities in the Twin Cities. The prospects looked promising, though they couldn't give him a firm answer.

After much discussion, on an enormous leap of faith we decided to say another "yes." Thanks to Macalester's flexibility with the start date, we gave ourselves six months to get ready to go.

I wish I could say that it was smooth sailing and pure bliss at every moment from accepting the job offer in late May to arriving at that locked and frozen chapel door in early January, but that wasn't the case. I was going to a job in a great city with amazing resources, but I couldn't shed an insistent nagging that perhaps God was not in this move. I wondered if I should have paid more attention to the other things calling me—my marriage, my children, the people who had gone to great lengths to make a future at Carroll College possible for me, and even some new ventures that were coming my way from colleagues at Carroll just as I was negotiating my new salary and start-date. The nagging feeling was heightened by daily grumbling from my children and spouse who pinned their normal daily stress to the move.

As a person who looks for outside "signs" as assurance or confirmation when decisions I've made seem uncertain, I had no lack of contenders. We had trouble finding a house in Minnesota in our price range that didn't have buyers standing in line. Complicating things even more, we had unexpected trouble selling our old house in Wisconsin. It had already been on the market a long time when it finally sold to buyers who wanted to close on it very quickly. This meant that for the for the last six weeks of our time in Wisconsin, our family was forced to live in a temporary dwelling, campus housing, with all of our belongings in a frustrating pack-or-unpack limbo.

Have you ever tried to live out of boxes stacked high and wide, with three children for six weeks? In the barrage of questions hurled my way, I couldn't help but hear a blaming tone.

"Mommy, where are my swimming goggles . . . I need them for my lesson!" *We didn't label everything in the box, Christopher.*

"Mommy, where is the kitty litter? Peppie stinks." *We'll just buy some.*

"Do you know where the Acts commentary went, Lucy? I'm preaching on a text . . ." *JUST BORROW IT FROM THE LIBRARY!*

We were all in disarray, emotions included. I was trying to hold it together, to maintain my trust that this was the right decision. But there were moments when my papered-over emotions came unglued. I vividly recall one evening.

It was the night of the college's annual Christmas choir concert. In small-town Wisconsin, a free concert of gorgeous Christmas music packed in the crowds. The chapel held 1,200 and not a seat was available. My role in the concert was to read the Christmas narrative from Luke's Gospel. I knew this was my last time to attend this event. It was another ending like so many that fall.

I put on the one dress I had kept back from the grip of the moving truck that had already taken the lion's share of our things to Minnesota. I made my way from our campus house across the icy street to the chapel. Mark Ammott, the director of choral music, greeted me.

"Thank you, Lucy, for doing this every year. You do such a great job with the reading. We will miss your wonderful voice."

The exhaustion of the weeks prior suddenly broke through the flood-gates in a burst of tears. Fortunately the student choir manager had signaled Mark away for the sound check at that exact moment and he missed my deluge. It was a night of raw emotion for me. Something has always arrested my spirit when I experience the simple elegance of Christmas music. The promising hope of new life holds sway on my heart. That night, with all that was ending and with little certainty ahead, I barely made it through my reading intact.

When I returned at 10:30 p.m. to our house, Tom was still at a late church meeting. The sitter had managed to get the children in bed and when I checked, they were actually asleep. This was quite a feat for anyone and I paid the sitter well. I was just about to send her home when I suddenly remembered.

Just before I had gotten ready for the concert, the children and I had put a couple loads of laundry in the coin machines in the residence hall across the street from our house. To get there, we had to go across the slippery parking lot that abutted the campus center, down a set of steps, through the college snack bar, around a corner, and into the dorm's laundry room. I had looked and felt like a mama duck with her three ducklings, if ducks could carry plastic baskets heaped with clothes. Even our two-year-old was carrying one very small load of laundry in a plastic beach bucket.

"I help!" she had demanded.

The transport of clothes to the machine would have taken Tom and me about five minutes all told. But with Tom out for the evening and the children insisting on helping, it had taken well over an hour. The baskets tipped at least three times, treating the snack bar full of students cramming for finals with the spectacle of a laundry explosion featuring two of my bras, a pair of my nine-year-old's briefs, a couple dried up washcloths, and so much powdery detergent.

"Mommy, I carry," Anna had announced as she tried to hold onto the box of laundry soap, spilling it all over the floor, where it caked in a pool of splattered soda pop.

"Oh, Annie, you are such a good helper," I said as I gently tried to pry the box from her hands. When she started to protest loudly, attracting the attention of every student in the room, I decided to just hustle everyone the rest of the way, mess or no. By the time we made it to the laundry room, I was forcing myself to take deep breaths.

And now, at 10:30 p.m. with a temperature of 10 below and a wind-chill of negative 20, I suddenly remembered all that laundry still sitting damply in the machines across the street. It would be a long night. I asked the sitter to stay while I ran out to shift the first loads over to the dryers. When I returned, Tom was finally home. It was past midnight when we folded the last of the laundry. Even years later when it should be a funny memory, I still think of that night as the perfect emblem of all that was hard about that period. Those long December nights mirrored the dark nights of my soul, the shortening days holding never enough light to guide my path through this momentous change we were about to undertake.

Does one's vocation lead to peace or to disruption? Does the summoning of ministry lead into fullness of life or to depletion that gets filled by the Source of Life only? Even in a moment of clarity about the presence of the divine in one's life, like my experience on the hillside long ago, is there room for doubt about the message itself?

"Is it God?" the student asks. Johanna and Jim's questions are the right questions. When asking questions and seeking guidance for the direction of their lives, they don't let God—or me for that matter—off the hook. I tell them that I am so often reminded, just like my experience on the porch, that God is a God of surprises. God sometimes speaks the word, "go," and then, at other times, won't let go.

CHAPTER 4

Knocking on Doors

I HAD BEEN ON the job for about a month. At a transition meeting with my predecessor, Dr. Donald Meisel, we brainstormed a list of key campus contacts he thought might "open a few doors" for my work. Dutifully, I arranged lunches and coffee conversations with the suggested faculty and staff, some of whom had served on the search committee. People were quick to respond to my request for meetings. They were initially quite kind. But as I listened attentively to their concerns for the college and their ideas about the chaplaincy, I realized that the mixed messages from the search committee about my work had not evaporated in the eight-month lapse between my interview in April and starting in January. Along with the message that I shouldn't expect much response to my efforts because the campus was not interested in religion, I also heard concerns from staff about a great divide between the work they do and the work of the faculty. Student Affairs staff thought faculty viewed them as out-of-the-classroom babysitters, policing all the "perfectly normal, albeit crazy behaviors" of students. Such assumptions, stated or implied, both diminished the work of Student Affairs professionals as valued colleagues and also leveled unfair accusations about their commitment to developing the whole student in body, mind, emotion, and spirit.

I was sympathetic to the issues staff people raised. At Carroll College I had encountered very similar issues. It seemed to be a perennial problem with small colleges. What came as a surprise was the dissatisfaction with the college that came from faculty as well. The presenting issue that two faculty members voiced was concern about the change in my reporting line from the president to the dean of students. "The other chaplains of this College reported to the president," one distinguished faculty member said, "which elevated their role. They were our chaplains, chaplains to faculty and the alumni as well as the students." I was confused by the emotional intensity of his words, noting his face was flushed, eyes tearing. I had not assumed any such thing, either the diminishment of my role by being grouped more closely with others in student support, nor that a change in my administrative structuring would mean I would solely focus on students. After all, my official title was Chaplain to the College. Though I had the sense they were both supportive, the two faculty members' anger at the administration over this and several other concerns left me uncertain. I realized that they must respect me and trust me to feel comfortable enough to raise these issues. As the newcomer I was outside the political boiling pot. They seemed to see me as a non-judgmental colleague who would listen and respect them. I dutifully assumed this role, though the conversations were definitely more about their need to talk than they were about welcoming or hosting me.

A few days after that meeting, I sat in a café down the block from my office with another faculty member. The view from through the plate glass window across from me was of six feet of snow; there was promise of more that night. This was the fifth lunch I had arranged since arriving. Jeff, my lunch companion that day, had received tenure a few years before. He was a geography professor. "I came to Macalester thinking it was a progressive place. You may have been told the same thing. We have great students but the administration is simply awful. When I got tenure, my colleagues basically told me to check out, which I took to mean, bury myself in research and keep a low profile on campus committees." I sat staring, trying to stave off the sinking feeling that was dragging me down. "If another option came along, I would be *so ready* to bolt from this scene," Jeff said. I lifted a spoonful of my now-cold chili. His words plunged me into an icy deep freeze. When we left the restaurant, I thanked him for his time. He pulled his knit cap over his ears, his glasses fogged up, and walked away without a goodbye.

As you can imagine, these lunches with faculty and staff were not drawing my most robust energy, to say the least. Did every faculty member at this college share this sense of frustration? Was the whole campus suffering from deep-seated dissatisfaction? The students too? From my first encounter with Macalester students in the interview, I had been quite taken with their fresh energy, humor, and readiness to challenge—the whole package. But since the unanticipated visit from Nathan on my first day, I'd met very few students.

So when, at my first official meeting with my new boss, Ed, suggested a *student-led* campus tour, I leapt at the idea.

I was sitting across from Ed at the cherry-wood table in his office, on a straight-back college insignia armchair. His eyes gazed up to catch a thought that was arriving. I couldn't tell whether he was thinking aloud to himself or speaking to me when he said, "I wonder if a campus tour is a good idea. Yes, yes, that might work."

At the time, I didn't know what response he expected. But as I came to discover over the next years working with Ed, this was just the way he conversed with me. He was a formal person, and indirect in his approach. I was unaccustomed to such. Growing up in a family that was very direct, sometimes jarringly so, there was no guesswork to communication. At home, I always knew the score. With Ed, I had to work my way into his thinking, hook the thought, reel it in, and then once it was in front of me, figure out whether it was a keeper or if I should cast it off to someone else. But that day, I realized it was intended for me.

"Having just arrived," he went on, "you might appreciate knowing your way around."

Later I wondered if Ed, an anthropologist by training, may have thought a campus tour would give me a clear perspective on the college. Whatever his motivations, I didn't care. I just wanted to meet some students. He called the Admissions Office and set up the tour.

"Yes, they can take you right away," Ed said, as if arranging a doctor's appointment.

I took my planner from my new leather tote and looked studiously at the pages. I knew full well I had nothing scheduled after my meeting with Ed, but I wanted to appear busy.

I left Ed's office and set out across the frosty sidewalks to meet the tour guide. I had been on numerous campus tours over my career as chaplain and my experience told me that it would probably give me a campus overview of the dining hall, snack bar, gym, classroom buildings, and the like. Any parent or anyone who works on a college campus, particularly admissions personnel, knows that a campus tour can be a deal breaker in the college search process for prospective students. I didn't have a deal to break, or a deal to make for that matter. I was the new chaplain of the college, just trying to learn whatever I could about my new community.

As I walked towards the admissions office, I thought about another campus tour I had taken when I interviewed for my position at Carroll

College some years earlier. That time, my student tour guide had also been a member of the search committee that hired me. I remembered little about our conversation but I did recall one of the places she took me on the tour. Though not part of the "routine" tour route, she unlocked the door to the college's "chapel." To anyone else's eye this room looked more like a massive auditorium, seating over 1,500—the largest gathering space on campus. I tried to align this echoey space with my usual idea of a chapel as intimate and human-sized but simply could not. My guide explained that the space needed to be that big because of an annual lecture series that was required for all students. When we turned to leave, instead of walking back outside, my guide led me up a back staircase and to another smaller chapel, no bigger than a large coat closet.

"This is the meditation chapel," she proudly declared. "This space is where I feel closest to God on this campus."

"Closest to God?"

"Well, there is something so quiet about it. It's close by but also out of the way. When I feel tense, I come here and just pray."

Her love for this little broom-closet of a chapel was evident and I was touched by this student's decision to share with me the place she thought of as her spiritual home on campus. She had not only let me into the back room of that building, but she had ushered me into her life as a student.

As I entered the Macalester College admission's office, I had my hopes up that something similar would happen this time. Any map could tell me the names of the buildings. What I wanted was a sense of the place itself and how the students—or at least the one assigned to the tour—actually lived in it. The office was like so many other admissions offices I had been in: the period wing-back chairs, a hutch with a few old college yearbooks and a trophy or two (placed there I guessed to remind prospective athletes that they could join a winning team by enrolling). The glossy brochures shimmered with photos: the campus lit by autumn's blaze, a group of smiling students engaged with a bearded faculty member in what appeared to be a very intense, intellectual conversation.

A young woman was chatting with the receptionist and, hearing me come in, she turned and extended her hand confidently to me.

"I am Samantha. You must be Lucy."

"Yes I am."

"We don't have many tours at this time of year so I figured you were the person Dean DeCarbo wanted me to show around."

"You're right," I said, smiling under the scarf wrapped around my face.

She was dressed for winter tours with her down jacket, jeans, enormous "moon boots" and a long stocking cap that reached her waist. The only indication that she was actually a very slight young woman were her delicate pink gloves. She opened the door for me and we started out. As we sped along, she warned me that because of the cold, the tour would be "abbreviated." I didn't know quite what she meant.

We made our way over the ice-glazed sidewalks. As we passed each building, Samantha pointed them out, telling me their names and what academic disciplines were housed inside them. Through chattering teeth she told me a few stories associated with the buildings, and some factoids like the number of volumes in the library. One of the buildings we went by had scaffolding on the outside. I inquired about it.

"That is Old Main, built in 1904. It was falling down, so they finally found the money to renovate it." She added, "The campus center over there," she pointed across the snow-covered lawn to a brick building with paint chipping off the window frames, "is slated for the wrecking ball sometime in the future."

I caught a note of sarcasm in her voice.

"Oh yeah, and they want to build a new gym. I am not a fan of tearing down these old buildings," she stated emphatically. "We—students—love the funky, beat-up and comfy feel of these places." She glanced over toward me and giggled. "Where else could we literally paint a floor for an event and not get in trouble for it?"

I was impressed with Samantha. She had a refreshing edge to her perspectives. Her take on the campus was clear, no bullshit. If it was also a bit clipped, I wrote this off as the cold-weather abbreviation she had warned me about.

She took me past other buildings—the science buildings, the art and humanities complex. We passed the gym and field house, residence halls and the chapel, which she didn't mention. I wondered why she didn't acknowledge the chapel. Perhaps she figured I knew what it was, since I worked there.

As we walked on, she ticked off the names of the buildings like clockwork: Dayton, Carnegie, Olin, Rice, Janet Wallace, Weyerhaeuser Hall. I wanted to ask about the people for whom these buildings were named.

I figured Dayton was connected with the Minneapolis-based Dayton-Hudson department store. I also knew that Macalester had just received a bucket-load of money after the *Readers Digest* stock had gone public. Its founder, DeWitt Wallace, was the son of a former Macalester president. Of course I knew the name Carnegie and saw on the engraved marquis that this was Carnegie Science Building, not unlike similar Carnegie-endowed science buildings on other campuses. But I didn't ask Samantha about the names because I thought she was in a big hurry. She was shivering, speeding toward Grand Avenue, a main arterial that divides the campus between the academic buildings and the dorms.

She pointed to the health services building as we passed.

"I'll drop you at the cafeteria. It's called Kagin," Samantha said. Then, "Oh, I almost forgot," she said, reaching into her pocket. "Here is your lunch ticket. The college would love to treat you to lunch. We do it for all our visitors."

Visitors? Does she think I was a visitor? I brushed my confusion aside, deciding that she was letting me in on a practice I could extend to the people *I* hosted at Macalester.

As we made our way into Kagin Commons, the lunch rush was underway. The sudden warmth, combined with the smell of institutional food, a wafting tang of greasy burgers and fries mingled with the residual bacon and eggs still lingering from breakfast, made me squint. The entryway was littered with backpacks, cigarette butts, and a sweatshirt tossed in a corner. A couple of dropped pens lay in puddles of mud and snowmelt. Samantha pointed the way up two different staircases to the food lines.

"This way you get grilled food. That way, you get meat, potatoes, daily features and the like. Standard fare. Nothing great. The food is . . . fine." She paused, checking her watch. "So, that's it." Clearly on autopilot, she turned to leave.

Seeing her turn to leave, I felt suddenly panicked. I had thought this tour might help me get a little more insight into the students at Macalester. What I had wanted were some clues about how students made connections and where they felt at home. Beneath these questions were my own questions, of course. How would I find my way into this place? Into students' lives? Into the soul of this college? I had enjoyed the tour but didn't expect it to be over so fast. I hadn't even gotten a chance to ask any questions. A feeling of disappointment began to wash over me. When would be my next chance to meet a student who might help me understand this place? If a person who was literally getting paid to tell me about the campus couldn't help me, who could? I decided to give it one last shot.

Samantha had greeted a friend outside the cafeteria. She was starting out the door but I managed to catch her.

"Samantha, before you go, I have a question for you," I said. She had just pulled on the hat she had removed when we came into the dining facility.

"Sure," she said. I knew she was in a hurry, so I went for the question I most wanted an answer to, the one that had made me feel so welcomed into student life at Carroll.

"In which building or space on campus do you feel most at home?"

The question seemed to catch her off guard. For the first time since we began the tour, she made direct eye contact with me. She stopped still for a moment. I paused and waited for her response.

"Wow, I haven't really thought about that before. Just a second . . ." She turned to greet another young woman coming in to get lunch. "Okay, sorry, what did you ask me?" I could tell my question had thrown her off, but I decided to persevere.

"I am just curious, where do you feel most at home here at Macalester . . . in what space, building?" She paused, tugging on her hat, her glove pointing out the door toward the other side of campus.

Finally, she answered. "Well, I really like the library. It's quiet. You can find spaces that are out of the way. One of the study rooms up on the top floor lets you look out over the whole campus and it's really nice. I don't know . . ." Her answer trailed off, as if she wasn't sure if she'd given me enough of an answer or too much of one.

Not looking at me, she said she needed to finish up because she had "stuff to do." I wondered if my question had made her uncomfortable.

"Oh yeah, I forgot to show you the dorms," she said. Pointing through the plate-glass windows to a cluster of buildings she ticked off the names: "Doty, Dupre, Wallace, Bigelow."

"Where do you live?" I asked.

"Oh, off campus. I *had* to get out of the dorm . . . too close to people." She seemed to wait for my response. I smiled and decided to back off. She had given me the distinct impression that she was finished with the tour. I then said, "Yes, I imagine it can be challenging to live in close quarters with your peers."

"Anything else?" she asked.

"I guess not."

She started to walk off, and I interjected: "Thanks for showing me around, Samantha."

"Sure," she said, glancing back, briefly. I watched her dart off toward the admissions office.

I stood alone in the dining hall entry, where groups of students were now pouring in. Most of them looked like they had just rolled out of bed, stubbing out their first cigarette of the day in the ashtray near the entrance, dropping heavy backpacks against the walls.

I was still holding the meal pass. There was something about the morning that had left me cold, unsettled. Was it the tour? Was it Samantha's style? Having just spent almost five years at a small-town college, students there simply didn't exude the confidence I encountered in Samantha. Maybe I just wasn't yet used to this kind of urban collegiate panache? I certainly couldn't criticize the way she conducted the tour. She was a pro. Able, practiced, Samantha did her job well. She knew the lay of the land. She wasted no time, a blessing on this sub-zero morning: "This is this and its function is that." It had certainly been a functional tour.

As I puzzled over my unsettled feeling, it dawned on me that she had not taken me inside any buildings except to drop me off at the dining hall. She had been thorough, but she had offered me only the outside view of the place. I suddenly realized how much Samantha's comment about it being for visitors had thrown me. I thought she knew I was the new chaplain—the fact that she had not bothered to point out the chapel building had seemed to indicate this, but maybe I had interpreted it wrong. Or maybe she knew I wasn't a visitor but had just referred to the ticket that way in her rush?

As I thought about this, still holding the meal ticket, I suddenly remembered our introduction in the admissions office. We had only used first names and I had never mentioned that I was the new chaplain. Without knowing who I was, from her perspective I was simply another guest on this campus—to her mind, an outsider. No wonder my question about where she felt at home may have seemed a little too personal, too close.

I noticed one of the students in the cafeteria line was eyeing me curiously. I realized I was just standing there in the entryway, twisting a meal ticket and staring blankly into the dining hall. I pulled myself out of my thoughts.

Don't overthink it, Lucy. I curbed my usual over-processing tendency and I considered which staircase to ascend for lunch—grill or regular fare? I decided neither, turned and went out the door.

I made my way back across the street. Snow had begun to fall again. I stepped in through the front door of the chapel, empty, silent. I paused and looked out the large plate glass windows onto the snow-covered campus. The American and United Nations flags flapped awkwardly on the prominent pole in front. I couldn't shake my unsettled feelings. I knew I was worried about my family in this new place. I had my own sense of inadequacy for the enormity of the work. But it was something more. Though I could have read my unsettledness as the urge to bolt from this place, I realized that it was actually the opposite: I wanted very much to go inside the buildings, to enter the lives of the students I had seen in line at the cafeteria, of my tour guide Samantha, of the faculty I'd met for coffee. My deep desire was not just to learn the names of the buildings but to get a sense of what the people they were named for had loved about this campus, having been devoted enough to make a building-worthy contribution. I was ready to investigate what made this place tick. I'd done it in other settings where I'd worked, but at this time, in this place, it seemed more challenging.

The tour had led me to a startling reflection: I am not an outsider. But I am also not an insider. And it suddenly occurred to me—would I ever be fully an insider on this campus or any other? Did I even want to be? Thinking about my role this way helped me understand that part of a chaplain's job is to see the campus from the outside while also engaging the inner life of its members. We need to be inside and outside at the same time. Our role makes us, in a way, a guardian of thresholds. By standing in neither place, and both, we can better recognize moments of important transition in the spiritual lives of our communities and place ourselves to help others move from one important space or moment into the next.

It was my own chaplain who had taken me to the threshold of a spiritual awakening more than twenty years earlier. It was on a late fall morning, a morning that started innocently enough with a visit to a campus coffee shop. That day brought me to the door that opened on what would ultimately become my vocational path.

I began college in 1971 under the shadow of the Vietnam War, four years after Martin Luther King, Jr. was assassinated, and at a time when issues of race, gender, and class were taking people into the streets to demand change. I enrolled at the same college my two older brothers had attended, Sioux Falls College. The year I arrived, there was a new college chaplain. He was a newly minted pastor, having just finished his Master of Divinity degree from a seminary in Berkeley, California. I cannot fathom the culture shock he and his wife must have experienced moving from 1971 Berkeley to Sioux Falls, South Dakota. Even as someone who grew up in un-hip Iowa, I knew that the 70s young adult cultural movements were taking their cues from California. The music, the lifestyles, the drug culture, the race riots, the war protests, even the Jesus Freaks, were all intimately tied to the Northern California scenes our chaplain came from.

I had the great fortune of meeting Larry early in our time at the college through my interest in the chapel program. I was a musician and I offered to play my guitar at the services he was launching. I quickly discovered his wit, his intelligence, and his interest in my development. This last quality surprised me as I thought he was so brilliant that I must have seemed quite banal to him. He became a gracious mentor to a young woman who had a questing, persistent heart.

The day that heart found itself at a new threshold was a November morning in my junior year. I had come to find a cup of coffee and a muffin after my early morning class. When I entered the college snack bar, I saw Larry sitting in the corner with a newspaper in hand. He was often there, usually conversing with someone—a returning Vietnam veteran, a member of the cross-country team or perhaps a faculty member. I approached him and he greeted me: "Sit down, if you have time."

I placed my order and joined him.

That day, not unlike others, began with a little small talk—the unexpected snow the night before, his wife's pregnancy. After a moment, Larry paused, and with a tilt of his prematurely balding head, looked up. He pointed his long angular finger at the nearby speakers and said, "What do you think Dylan is saying in this song?" I stopped in my tracks. A tremor went through my body like I'd brushed against a ghost. I hadn't even noticed the song playing in the background that had accompanied my entrance to that space, our conversation. I listened again, more closely. The tinny voice came with force: "Knock, knock, knocking on heaven's door . . ." The shiver made my stomach churn. As I sat across the table from my chaplain I felt a sensation that was utterly new, and yet as familiar as the aroma of the coffee wafting up from the cup I held. It was a rush of joy, like someone had opened a door to and invited me to enter a grand party, an odd contrast to this gray, steely winter morning. Right there in the campus coffee shop, he was asking me to consider what it meant to be knocking on heaven's door.

With his eyes squarely on mine, he said, "Bobby Dylan . . ." (his voice had an uncharacteristic tremor as he said the name, as if he realized the intimate way he referred to this musical icon) ". . . has a prophet's gaze on the world, Lucy."

My mind raced. My introduction to adulthood was coming at a time of massive eruptions of race and gender tensions. Our country was embroiled in a war that we couldn't extricate ourselves from gracefully. I had friends who had died in it, and brothers who worried they would too. Vietnam veterans were returning to campus on the GI Bill, fresh from their tours of duty, their once-short hair now hanging down their backs in ponytails, their fatigues looking, well, fatigued. They were the quiet ones on campus.

It was a momentous time even on that tiny campus in Sioux Falls. Just a few weeks before, the large caricature of a Native American brave that stood in front of the college's student union announcing the college's homecoming activities was burned. No one claimed responsibility for it, but we all knew it was a statement on the disrespectful representation of Native people.

I didn't know then that the 1970s was a time that scholars of culture call "hinge times." These are dynamic cultural moments when the old order is no longer adequate to hold the emerging issues but the new order has yet to arrive. Though I didn't have language for it at the time, I felt strongly that not only I but the whole world was standing at a threshold. Maybe that's what Dylan was saying. I heard in his lyrics my own impulse to ask, to plead, to hold open the way for something to emerge from all the erupting life around me.

That day I remember trying to articulate to Larry how I felt but was frustrated by my inability to articulate it. Hundreds of questions erupted from that opening, questions like: *Is God knocking on the door of the world? How do we let God in? Are humans pleading for God's help in the middle of the problems that beset the world? And am I supposed to do something to help make the world a better place to live? Is God knocking on the door of my heart?* These and other questions were close to the surface, but that morning, I was so overcome I couldn't speak. It is a good reminder that there are times when the most profound insight takes a while to form. The seed takes time to form into a full blossom.

I held these thoughts and questions and later on, as I was wont to do, I pulled out my journal notebook and scrawled a little entry. I had never thought about the word before, but an "entry" is exactly what it was. Scribbling my thoughts was a way of entering the door into a vast universe of ideas, of relationships. Whether or not I had the wherewithal to knock on heaven's door and reach for the door handle, at that very high moment, I would have sold my soul to whoever was on the other side of it, if it had opened.

The thrill of that awakening had never left me. Just as my own chaplain had done for me, I wanted to provide a sense of belonging for young people who found themselves at a major life transition. He had not only set my eyes on a vast universe in the course of a casual conversation, but a few months later, he gave me the encouragement to begin what would become the central path of my life.

On the college quad, a few days after he had announced he'd be leaving the college to pursue graduate study, he stopped me on my way to class. It was in the middle of another seemingly innocuous conversation that he suddenly tapped my heart with the words, "I think you'd make a fine college chaplain, Lucy." I remember my disbelief when he said it. I thought I could never be a chaplain like him. But perhaps seeing my uncertainty, he then said, "Lucy, you should just go to seminary. Just go. The direction will come once you are there."

Those words came back to me as I stood looking out on the snowy quad at Macalester after my disappointing morning tour. Just go. Just take the step and direction will come. His advice remained as powerful twenty years later as it had when I was a young woman, longing for direction. Perhaps the longing to be a part of this community was the new direction I needed to trust would come to me. Instead of looking for my cues to come from external approval, maybe I should allow my urge to belong, that is, to be established as a community citizen, guide my vocational feet. I wanted *in* with all my being, as urgently as I had wanted that locked door to open a few weeks before. Though Samantha may have thought I was a visitor, an outsider, I was ready to step over the thresholds of this college, to tend the souls of students, faculty, staff. I wanted to look them in the eye, listen to their dreams, their worries, their fears, to notice where their gazes rest, to learn what breaks their hearts. I yearned to receive and launch them.

Remembering my chaplain's advice felt like my first step towards figuring out how to enter the heart of the community I had been hired to care for. I had to trust that my desire to serve them in this way would be the very key to letting me reach them.

Turning from the window, I went down the stairs to my office. I was already regretting not having gotten lunch at the campus center and thinking about where I might get a sandwich. As I arrived at my door, I saw it: a folded paper taped to the handle.

I opened the note. It was from a student I had met at a church in Wisconsin just before I moved and who had recently started at Macalester. Quite honestly, I had forgotten about her. The note was an invitation for me to join her at a gathering of her women's spirituality group. She said she had loved meeting me at her church in Waukesha and thought some of the other women might enjoy connecting.

This invitation would change the entire course of my work at this college.

CHAPTER 5

Going Inside

THE INVITATION COULDN'T HAVE come at a more welcome moment. As I found out later, the student women's spirituality group was called Threads: Weaving Together Our Lives and had been founded the previous fall by a group of women, including the student I had met in Wisconsin. The group met weekly. I called the number on the note and didn't hear anything back until the afternoon a few days later when the student who had invited me suddenly appeared outside my office.

"We are a feminist gathering," the young woman explained, standing in my doorway. "I am not sure if you know, but in a feminist gathering we have a flat organizational structure. Everyone is equal." I resisted the urge to tell her that I had cut my teeth on feminist organizational theory.

"We meet in one of the Three Little Pigs," she said, gesturing toward one of the chapel doors. "Oh?" I said. Seeing my confusion she explained, "That's what we call the three cottages across the street from campus." She gave me the specifics of the meeting.

As she turned to leave, I thanked her again for inviting me. "Yes, I am really excited to come," I said.

A few nights later, I made my way to the specific "pig" she had designated. Immediately upon entering, it became clear that "pig" was a fitting nickname. From the kitchen I could hear a refrigerator on its last legs, maybe not oinking but squealing loudly. From another direction came a disturbingly loud moan. This turned out to be the toilet, letting out the sound it made every time it was flushed, starting shortly after the first feminist greeted me.

One of the students unrolled a woven runner with bold reds, yellows, and greens, placing it on the low coffee table. When I inquired about it, she proudly told me it had been a gift from her host family in Guatemala, where she had gone on study abroad. As others arrived they "set the altar" with clay candleholders, a little goddess statue, a cross inlaid with lovely stones, a feather, a carved box. One woman opened a bag and poured out a pile of small stones. Couches with stuffing spilling from threadbare cushions and straight-back chairs circled the table. Stained floor pillows and two beanbag chairs also received ready participants.

"Oh, we don't have any candles . . . does the chapel?" one of the women asked me.

I nodded and hopped up to fetch them. As I made my way to the door, one of the students introduced me to the others.

"This is Lucy, our new chaplain," she said. I said hello and the students smiled.

Just as I began to shut the door behind me, still pulling on my coat, I heard another student say, "Yeah, we haven't ever had non-students here but she seems cool."

I sped across the street and up the sidewalk to fetch my contribution, candles from the chapel. When I returned, I placed the half-burned candles (the best I could do) in the clay holders. One of the students pulled a lighter out of her pocket, her cigarettes tumbling after. Once lit, the glow of the flames swallowed and transformed the shabby space. The reflected fire ignited in the eyes of each student around the altar and we sat there for the longest time, in silence.

These glowing moments on the quiet and peace of a winter night soon gave way to an hour of incredibly intense sharing. I shouldn't have been surprised, given the evening's topic: "Women and Violation." One student began with two quotes by Adrienne Rich: "The connections between and among women are the most feared, the most problematic, and the most potentially transforming force on the planet."[1] And then, "When a woman tells the truth she is creating the possibility for more truth around her."[2]

The two student facilitators stated their intent clearly: "By telling these stories, we break the silence of those who have been silenced . . . give voice to those who are voiceless." Then one facilitator invited the group to tell stories, either our own or the stories of those we knew who had experienced

1. Rich, "Disloyal to Civilization," 279.
2. Rich, "Women and Honor," 193.

violation. After each person shared her story everyone was invited to take a stone from the pile on the table. We were instructed that later, when we felt the weight of the stone or pulled it out of its place, we were to remember the person and the story.

We began with silence, but I was struck by its ease. It wasn't a tense silence, desperately waiting for someone to fill it. This silence was comforting. I found myself moved by this circle of young women, sitting in a darkened room with flames dancing in their eyes. After a few minutes, the student facilitator gave a prompt: "Have you ever met someone who has experienced abuse in a relationship or by a stranger?"

One student began. She told a very sad story of a friend whom her roommate's brother sexually assaulted when he was visiting for the weekend at the college. She collected her stone. Silence. The next speaker was a woman who had been assaulted when on study abroad by the father of her host family. She collected her stone and we in turn took one but this time there was no silence. Three more stories followed rapidly, of those in the circle and friends they knew. The pile of stones quickly shrank. I was stunned by the number of women in that group who had been raped or abused in relationships both prior to and during college.

That night I was a fellow traveler with them, all of us looking over our shoulders to times of innocence in our past, to a moment of fear and shock and the added stress of finding ourselves with few resources, to realizing that we were not the first women to hold each other against fear and worry and wondering what would come next. The conversation in the room that night extended as far back as women have sat in circles by fires, to ancient times. In our candle fire we glimpsed our foremothers—some whose names we didn't know and others whose names were known around that circle.

But that night I also entered another sanctum, not unlike my previous college's little closet chapel, shared with me by a student. I experienced a spiritual connection with the other women in the room. Our simple circle became a setting where the holy arose from declarations of trauma, from isolating experiences of rape and violation. These horrors should never happen to anyone. But that night, we stepped on the holy ground of grace within our circling candles, and I sensed that the ground held healing and hope.

I thought of the biblical story of Ruth, Orpah, and their mother-in-law, Naomi, on the plains of Moab, three widows in a foreign country, not knowing where to go, having lost everything familiar, looking down a road to a severe wilderness. They must have thought about how things could have been different. "If only our husbands hadn't died, here in this far-off land. If I had stayed close to home and married the one my father had in mind, I might have had a future," the women on that Moabite plain might have been thinking.

I heard many of these what-ifs come forward from the students as well:

"If only I hadn't gone to that party . . ."

"I heard he was creepy but I thought it was just bad chemistry between that one girl and him . . ."

"Yes, I did drink too much . . . I don't remember what happened exactly . . . I woke up naked."

In fleeting moments, their trust shattered, life was rent asunder.

But around the circle that night I also detected the spirit of the Moabite women. Ruth's words as she spoke to her mother-in-law Naomi echoed in their bruised spirits: "Where you go I will go, where you lodge I will lodge . . . your people will be mine . . . your God my God" (Ruth 1:16). These amazing students didn't necessarily know that they were carrying the courage handed to them by Ruth, Naomi, and even Orpah, who turned away from her sister-in-law and her mother-in-law to return to her home.

But what I marveled at was the students' determined arms reaching for each other, holding one another's pain and possibility both in the room that night and later, in the form of the slender stones we slipped into our purses, packs, pockets.

That night I did something I'd never done with students before. I told them the story of my own rape experience. Beforehand, I spent a long time debating whether I should speak or not. Doing so would represent a huge break in the rigid professional boundaries I usually kept with students. As I sat there, a million questions ran through my mind: Would telling them my story confuse my relationship with them? Would they feel like they needed to take care of me? Would I be drawing undue attention to myself, my life, my experience? Though I entered this group as a participant I realized that no matter the setting, I am a chaplain. This often happens in settings on campus and off, when the multiple roles of participant, group member, board chair, church attender, parent, spouse, all carry the freight of my call as a spiritual leader. I let all the questions have their say and decided that the gift of their invitation to share needed to be honored. Like Naomi looking into Ruth's eyes and seeing her deep devotion and willingness to venture into the unknown future, I looked into the eyes of these students and knew I needed to journey with them into a new place.

After this moment of silence (that held so many questions), I decided to speak. They were talking about the most vulnerable experiences of their lives and in this context of trust and deep care I sensed that they would welcome this disclosure. I told them because I was, and continue to be to this day, convinced that ministry at its heart is *about* the heart. There are times on this planet when hearts break, and that night I wondered if God's heart was breaking as each story tumbled out, like stones churning under the surf.

Looking around at the candle-lit faces, the circle gently swaying as some women rubbed the back of the friend next to them, I told them my story.

I had gone out to Washington State to work as an intern for the Presbyterian Church the summer between my first and second year of seminary. In that job I took high school kids to state parks and led campfire programs for weekend campers. It was very low-key evangelism. I told the women around the circle about the gorgeous August day toward the end of my internship, the air light and breezy, the mountains' snowy peaks glowing in the distance. I should have been outdoors enjoying the beauty of the day, I told them, but though I wasn't after a grade, I needed to finish the final report for my summer's work and the church office had a typewriter I could use. The students smiled—either in understanding of a deadline or amusement over the idea of having to use a typewriter, I wasn't sure.

I explained that my good friend Ellen, who had been in Oregon working as a student hospital chaplain, was to arrive later in the week. We had planned to make a little cash doing a house-painting job before driving back to Princeton, New Jersey in time for classes to begin.

It was after lunch that I stopped by the church to finish my paper. The students' candle-lit faces grew sober when I said that I had no idea that on this day, my life, my faith, my assumptions about my career direction, everything that I trusted, cared about and embraced would be shattered.

I mentioned to them that the church was empty. The custodian who had been outside the secretary's office that morning, doing the usual floor scrubbing and polishing, had left. The roofers who had been patching a leak seemed to be gone for the day. I didn't tell them about the smell of mimeographing fluid that filled the office from the freshly printed weekly worship bulletin, but it's a detail I've never forgotten. My voice shook and my hands trembled as I reminded them and myself how impossible it would have been to guess that the only interest of the man then pulling into the church driveway was to inflict deep harm. His life narrative is inconsequential except that it led him to be a serial rapist. And I was one on a long list of victims.

I noted that I dimly remember hearing the squeak of boots on the linoleum of the hallway leading from the parking lot through the open office door. I didn't share the fact that I was wordsmithing the document in the typewriter, and was so engrossed that I was only half aware that someone was standing there. I did say that I turned from my typing and I saw blue jeans and a white shirt with a jacket, that I glanced up at him and said in my inviting, hospitable way, "May I help you?"

I chose not to tell them that he ordered me to take my clothes off, that I thought I hadn't heard him right until I realized he was holding a pocket knife half-opened in his hand, or that when I saw the knife, my heart leapt in my throat. In the other stories that evening, many had said they wanted to cry or scream out. That afternoon, I was acutely aware that there was no one around to hear me, even if I had dared to scream. All of the students spoke of feeling dizzy, sick, and horrified during and after the assault. Most said aloud what I had thought that afternoon: "He is going to kill me."

I did share a bit more of the story, though not all of it. I didn't tell them that I took my clothes. As I did, he shut and locked the office door. I took everything off, asking compliantly, "Where do you want me?" I remember starting to shake violently. I kept some details to myself: leaning against the handles of the cabinets, preparing myself for what was to be my first sexual experience, the shock of his unzipped pants, how stunned I was. Though I didn't describe them to the students, as I spoke I was remembering his eyes, his face, his words: "Don't look at me."

I didn't mention that the most shattering experience of my life took about five minutes. I did tell them that I thought about what was next, that I remembered the knife. I also told them that I uttered a prayer to God at that moment and said, *Okay, God, this is it. I don't want to die!* I don't remember if I told them about the very odd feeling that came over me, how I felt intensely sorry for this man, and how I prayed that if I died, if he killed me, that somehow my life would mean something to someone.

Of course, as the students knew by the very fact of my sitting there, telling the story twenty years later, that I hadn't been killed. Rather, he zipped up and started to flee. But then on his way out the door he turned, saying, "If you call the cops, I will come back and kill you."

I didn't mention the harsh footsteps echoing back down the hall. I did tell them that I put my clothes on shakily and waited twenty minutes or so before leaving the church office, utterly unsure of what I should do next.

That night with the students I stopped there, though there was more to the story. The students were wide-eyed, some tearful, some staring at the floor, most reaching for a stone. I looked down at my hands. My fingers were wrapped around the stones I'd taken earlier. I simply held them, gently. I waited for the convener to speak. She asked if anyone else wanted to share. When no one else did we all stood and in a moment of spontaneity, we melted into the warm embrace of a circle hug. As the students stepped out into the cold winter night, they were held not only with the steady arms of their friends, but I sensed, the everlasting arms of One who won't let go. It takes brave companions along the way to traverse the rough roads, the fear, the pressing aloneness. I know what it means to receive care from others. I have put myself in a role where I am constantly learning what it means to give it.

Hearing the stories of hurt, harassment, exploitation, and in this case, sexual abuse, is one of the practices of ministry. I have long known that a vital act of caring for others is simply listening to them tell the stories they need to tell. But that night, but I learned something new about another way to minister. Opening up my own veins of fear, worry, pain and vulnerability with students provides ways to grow in my own vulnerability, a quality that is so central to the life of faith. This was a new model of ministry to me. Most of the clergy I'd known seemed so in control, never showing much emotion except when they were shouting from the pulpit. They might tell stories about sin and evil in their hearts but it didn't seem connected to their daily life or connected to the struggles of those with whom they were ministering.

The story I told the students that night was only the beginning of a story that continues to this day.

That August afternoon, as soon as I heard his car roar out of the parking lot, I quickly went to office door and locked it. I sat naked, stunned, shaking. I thought, "Yes, this is a church office. Yes this is a church. No, what I think just happened should not have happened. And for some reason, I am still alive." I looked at the phone. *Should I call someone? No, he'll for sure come back and finish what he started. He said he'd kill me.* I was too terrified to consider whether or not this was actually likely. A million shrieking voices each with their own demand for action teemed in my dazed head. *What if the car I heard roar out of the parking lot belonged to someone else? Was he still lurking in the shadows, around the hall corner? In the church nursery? Would he really return to kill me if I told someone?* Though he was probably miles away by then, I remained frozen, convinced that this man would follow me, would finish what I assumed had he set out to do that day—to inflict more violence. He couldn't have been clearer: if I told anyone what had happened, I would die.

And then the question arose, *Who would I even tell?* Amid my fear, a new realization coldly dawned on me: *Oh, wow, I have no one to tell, to call.* He had specifically said he'd kill me if I called the police, so they were the most terrifying of all the possibilities that flitted through my mind. My local host family? My relationship with them was already awkward—the idea of reporting anything remotely sexual was more than I could imagine. My parents? I didn't want to worry them and besides, they'd probably want to call the police, which I'd already decided was a death sentence. My friend Ellen might understand but I didn't know how to reach her. I also didn't want to drag her into this—if he did decide to come back, she would be just as vulnerable as me. On that bright August afternoon, I was entirely alone.

As I drove home after the warmth of that Threads Women's Spirituality circle, I found myself thinking, not about the attack itself, but about the fear and isolation I felt afterwards. One of the most devastating moments in the most devastating hours of my life was when I realized that I had no one to turn to for support.

The story I shared with students that night goes a long way in explaining why I feel so passionately called to work with young women. I love empowering women to find their fullness and to be fully engaged in life. This is the aspect of my work that has at its core a sense of justice as I work to counteract some of the inequalities experienced by women all over the world. My own experience of sexual violence at a young age, and the fact that it happened in a church, eventually ignited in me a passionate and raging energy in my life.

That night, after hearing the stories of so many young women who, like me, had felt alone and frightened in the aftermath of an attack, I realized with new conviction that part of my work as a chaplain was to make sure young adults have someone to be with them in their fear, to support them in their care for each other, to offer a steady hand to guide them when theirs shake. In 1976, I had no idea that I would spend my future career face to face with students whose experiences had so much in common with what I had encountered alone in that church office. There's no question that there is a danger to over-identifying with those to whom you minister. They are not you and you are not they. But I also cannot escape the fact that I know what it is like to be young, alone, scared, and needing someone who might understand, even a bit.

A few weeks after the Threads circle, I unlocked my office door to a ringing phone. My boss, the dean of students, was on the other end of the line.

"Lucy, I have a tough request for you," he said. "I just hung up from a student's mom calling with terrible news. She told me that her husband was killed in a car accident on his way to work. She's been trying to reach her son and can't seem to locate him. "

"Oh, how awful," I said.

"Yes, really, really tragic. Would you be willing to try to call this student? I'm sorry but I have to go to a very important meeting this morning."

"Of course I can."

"Thank you, Lucy. His name is Zach Pearson." He gave me Zach's dorm and phone number. "I know this will hard," he said, pausing. "Oh, and Zach doesn't seem to have a religious affiliation."

"Yes, it is no problem."

"Thank you, Lucy," he said, and hung up.

I looked out the window of my office, watching students rushing by on the sidewalk. It was a gleaming clear morning. The snow glimmered before my eyes like millions of diamonds. On any other day this scene would hold so much beauty and joy, but today, this day, this phone call I was about to make would change Zach's life. For him, snowy gleaming days might forever be associated with this one. I would have liked to go to his dorm room and deliver the message in person but the college discourages staff from going into the student residence halls unaccompanied. I paused before I picked up the phone.

"Enter this moment, O God."

That was all, just a little request arising from a moment of uncertainty. My hand trembled when I reached for the receiver and punched in Zach's room extension. The phone rang three times and a groggy voice answered.

"Hello. Is this Zach Pearson?" I asked.

"No. I'm Zach's roommate. He's here though, at least I think. Wait. No, he isn't. Can I have him call you?"

"Yes. I am Lucy Forster-Smith, the Chaplain. My number is 6293."

"Huh? Okay . . ."

The phone rang five minutes later. It was Zach.

"Hello. My roommate, Ben, told me someone called. Was it you?"

"Zach, yes, I am Lucy Forster-Smith, the new chaplain here at Macalester. I just received a call from the dean of students who said your mom has been trying to reach you. I have some very sad news. Zach, is there someone with you?"

"Yes."

"Zach, I am so sorry to tell you this over the phone, but your father died in a car accident."

Silence.

"Oh. Oh . . ." I heard a sob.

"I am so sorry, Zach." I held the silence.

"Zach, your mom needs to talk with you. I am here all morning. My office is in the lower level of the chapel. Please come over and see me after you talk with your mom."

Silence.

"Okay?" I ventured.

"Okay," he said before hanging up.

There are moments in life when time plays a dirty little trick of stretching endlessly, like a long road carrying a traveler to an unknown destination. On that morning, that road left me feeling lost and disoriented, imagining the conversation between Zach and his mom. I guessed that my phone call would be a turn in the road that for Zach was leading him to a far, unfamiliar country. A shiver made its way up my spine.

When I say I am a college chaplain most people I know assume my primary work is to counsel students. They must imagine me sitting in a wonderfully welcoming space, filled with cozy chairs, surrounded by the books that have guided me into this work, waiting for students to find me with their problems. I love the image and it is one that draws me in. But in reality, meeting with students individually actually comprises little of my overall time. Most of the time I am meeting with colleagues, dreaming up and carrying out student programs, preparing worship services, involved with community outreach and overseeing staff. Yet, the moments when I sit with students who are grieving, puzzling, worried, or celebrating are the times when I feel most like a chaplain. Often, this is when I am invited to enter lives at the moment they are most vulnerable. And those who come to speak with me request my ear, my eye, and most potently, my heart, to attend to their need. I know the deep importance of finding someone to talk with, someone who can be an anchor during the storms that rage when you are afraid or uncertain or feel very lost.

That day as I waited for Zach to come in to see me, I worried that I was inadequate for the task ahead. And actually, I think I was right to worry. Alone, indeed, I was inadequate. Who alone can hold such loss? I trusted God would be there.

When I heard heavy footsteps coming down the hall, I rose from my desk, and went to the door. I couldn't see Zach's face, which was hidden in the hooded depths of a gray Macalester sweatshirt, but I didn't need to see it to know that he was buried in grief. He was lost, unsure of which door was mine. I also reminded myself that he didn't even know who I was.

"Zach?"

His eyes didn't meet mine exactly. "I'm him."

"Come in," I said. I motioned for him to sit down on the couch in my office. I shut the door, gently. His large frame collapsed on the couch, filling my small space. Silence.

"Did you get hold of your mom?"

"Yeah, she called right after we hung up. I . . . I just can't believe it. . ."

Zach's voice dropped as if he was talking to himself.

"He was on his way to work and some bus slammed into his car. They think the bus driver missed a stop sign or something. Oh, God . . . I can't even think about it."

"Zach, I am so sorry, so, so sorry," I said, leaning forward.

Zach looked at the floor, head between his hands. After awhile he looked out the window and then down again.

"Chaplain, our family doesn't have much money. I have to get home to Florida. My mom asked if the college might be able to loan me some money. I'm sort of embarrassed. My mom is really upset."

"Zach, no problem. The chapel has funds for this kind of thing. I was going to tell you about it. Also the dean of students office will tell your professors what happened. Don't worry about the college stuff right now."

He nodded and we sat in silence again.

"I don't do emotions well," he admitted. "I guess it's the handicap of us scientists." I wasn't quite sure what he meant by "us scientists" but I sensed that he wanted me to know that he was holding in a lot.

"Yes."

I noticed his dim eyes, their dilated pupils staring over my shoulder, in the region of my eyes, but with no contact. His hands hung limp in his lap, shaking now.

"My mom gave me a number for the airlines but I guess I forgot it in my room."

"Zach, I am happy to get the airline's phone number." But it was clear he didn't hear me. The corner of his mouth tipped downward slightly, and a very gentle but audible sigh that came from someplace deep. He may not have heard it himself. I waited. He then caught my eye as he glanced my way.

"You may think this is weird but I had a dream a couple weeks ago. I can't remember much of it but what I do remember is that my dad was saying something to me but it was in a foreign language. I was so frustrated because I couldn't understand what he was saying." His face lit up for a moment. "Must be the Japanese class I just started—getting into my subconscious. I remember I kept asking him to repeat it, and he did and I still didn't understand. After a while, I just walked away because I was so frustrated. I then woke up and had this feeling that he was in my room. He seemed to have come from the dream. Oh, I don't know, but I think I was just hoping he might be there." He paused. "I was probably in one of those dream states. But when I thought he was there I thought I heard the faint words, and it was his voice saying, 'I love you, Zach.'" His eyes welled over and streams of tears ran down his cheeks. He kept his head down, eyes closed. When his nose bubbled, embarrassing him, I handed him the box of tissues.

For the next stretch of time, the only sounds in the room were soft sobs. I sat, holding silence as I had many times that hour—sometimes because I felt instinctively that it was what Zach preferred, more often because I simply didn't have the words. The view from my chair was that Zach was in a deep, trembling chasm. In this moment of profound grief, there was nothing I could do to accompany him except to maintain my steady presence. When he looked up, the air held our gaze.

"Sorry," he said.

That is when the tears arrived for me. The silence still held his words, and the room seemed flooded with such sadness that it was almost light. I felt like I could see sorrow and healing mix in the same instant, as Zach remembered the dreamed confirmation of his father's love even in the depths of profound sadness. His tear-filled eyes held that love. In that moment I witnessed the poignant grace of one who knew death, who wondered if he could go on and who, to his great surprise had received a deep and abiding gift.

"I wish I'd told him about it. We were really close," Zach said, wiping his cheeks. "It will never be the same without him." What could I say? We both knew he was right.

We arranged a flight out that afternoon. Zach's girlfriend and his roommate came by my office to see how Zach was doing and to pick him up to take him to the airport. I watched as the three of them walked down the hall, one friend on each side with their arms enveloping Zach. A long journey was ahead for all of them.

Though I had shared moments of deep grief with others before in my ministry I had never before been the first to break such news to someone. I found myself deeply shaken by facing the unspeakable grief of a child whose life would be forever changed. I had been granted the privilege of accompanying him over a threshold. For him there would be no turning back. Though I was powerless to rescue him from this new landscape of grief, at least I could help ensure that on the first steps of his journey toward healing, he was not alone.

CHAPTER 6

Opening Doors of Hospitality

IN TRYING TO UNDERSTAND how God courses through the story of my
life, it is often when I feel most helpless to do much of anything, to come
up with the right word, or to have the good sense to be silent when the situation demands it, that I am most aware of the holding love of God.

Presbyterian pastor, former chaplain, and writer Frederick Buechner opens his book *Alphabet of Grace* with these words, "At its heart most
theology, like most fiction, is essentially autobiography. Aquinas, Calvin,
Barth, Tillich, working out their systems in their own way and in their own
language, are all telling us the stories of their lives . . . Even at their most ce-
rebral and forbidding, you find an experience of flesh and blood, a human
face smiling or frowning or weeping or covering its eyes before something
that happened once."[1] The flesh and blood of ministry is presence, is one
human holding the heart of another.

In the case of the Threads Women's Group, it was a community who
joined to hold the hearts of one another. I had made a discovery that night:
that when I am vulnerable, sharing the pain and joy of my life with others,
deep and enduring relationships arrive. Perhaps it was a development I was
ready for in my personal life or maybe it was the beautiful receptivity of
this community of women, but I stepped over a wide chasm of fear that
night—fear of being rejected or labeled by the experience of rape. What I
came to discover was that when the members of a community hold their

---

1. Buechner, *Alphabet of Grace*, 1.

grief and joy in the presence one another, this enduring commitment to each other joins individuals into a beloved community.

I would also discover that part of my work as a chaplain is going inside my own heart, mind, soul and being brave enough to look at the complexities, the fear, the hurt, the joy, the marvels that erupt from my life. Part of being a minister is being willing to tell the truth about my life, and much of that truth is anchored in God's miraculous love, care, and grace that abounds.

I know there have been times in my life when I found myself without that love and grace. My terrible afternoon in a church office twenty years before was the start of a period of profound theological doubt, one that ironically coincided with my academic training to equip me for the ministry.

All of the seminary's neat, intellectually tight arguments for God's existence, presence, and power had walked out the door with that rapist. Where was the God I thought guided my every step? Where was the protector God I had been told would keep me from harm's way? A million questions erupted in the space of a milli-second.

I spent the week after the rape alone in the neighborhood where it had happened. I was in shock. All I wanted was someone to be with me. But all the people I knew locally—both the church pastor's family and the family I lived with—were away on vacation. I didn't want to worry my family who were in far-off Iowa. With no one to talk to, I went over the details of the rape in my mind again and again. It was my attacker's haunting last words to me, "If you call the cops, I will come back and kill you," that left the cold terror flowing through my veins.

When the pastor and his wife, Jack and Barbara, returned later that week, I went to their condominium and shared with them what had happened. They were shocked, but asked all the right questions. "Did you go to the hospital to be examined?" *No.* "Could you be pregnant?" *Probably not.* "Did you go to the police?" *No.*

"Nothing like this has ever happened before," I told them. "I didn't know what to do. I was all alone." I could hear the loneliness in my words but I didn't cry. I couldn't feel anything.

They encouraged me to talk with the police, to report the crime. Jack offered to go with me to make the report. The next day we drove down the hill from their condo to the police station. As we entered the building, I realized I'd never been inside a police station before. I was struck by the bars on windows, the sterility of white walls and metal desks, and by blue uniforms, badges, barricades. We told the intake officer behind a tall counter why we were there. He said that there was a woman officer who took these kinds of reports. I breathed a sigh of relief. Until I saw her.

She was unsmiling and rough in her affect. There was no greeting and she hardly looked at me as she barked questions like a mad dog, jotting answers down on a pad of paper. *Name? What happened? When? Where? Description.* It felt like an interrogation, as if I had been the one who had done something wrong. When I told her it had happened a week before, she was very angry. "How can you expect me to do my job if you don't report it right away? I need to find, prosecute, and jail these bastards," she said. I tried to explain that I had been alone, terrified that the rapist might have my car's license plate number, and I that didn't have a clue where the police station was. I told her about the rapist's threat that he'd come back and kill me if I reported it. She was unmoved by what she clearly saw as my gullibility.

That interview could not have ended too soon. Maybe I *had* been naive to believe his threat enough not to seek police help for a whole week, but her attitude only reinforced my feeling that I couldn't trust those who were supposedly there to help. Jack sat with me, pained, motionless, and when we left he simply gave me a tender squeeze on the arm. We both walked out of there knowing that the police's work was to "find, prosecute, and jail" the rapists. Yes, that was her work. But I realized the kind of help I needed was something much more than that.

I was experiencing what Sharon Daloz Parks aptly calls "shipwreck" experiences that "suddenly rip into the fabric of life or slowly yet just as surely unravel the meanings that have served as the home of the soul."[2] In moments like this, especially for young people who are still formulating and reformulating their understanding of the world, the experience of losing the framework that has previously given shape and meaning to life can be especially devastating. For college students, who are often away from their families for the first time and among peers who are not yet accustomed to the idea that they might have responsibility to be one another's caretakers, the experience can also be profoundly isolating. If they find themselves far from their trusted support system, even what one might consider a small crisis like a poor grade on an exam or challenges with roommates or friends

2. Parks, *Big Questions*, 39.

can throw them into a panic. When something as shattering as the death of a friend or family member or a personal experience of violation happens, the very ground of their being is shaken. Like the washed-up victim of a shipwreck, they may find themselves immobilized.

Very often, the experience of shipwreck leads to a period of asking the kind of unanswerable, deeply pained questions that quickly become questions about their faith. For me, in that late summer of 1976, these included: *Would I ever be able to be alone in a church or chapel again without thinking that when the door opened it could be an assailant? Would I never fully trust men again?* I would struggle for years to experience sexual expression as beautiful and holy. But what I really wondered is if God had a purpose for having me live through this terrifying experience.

A few weeks later, I took these questions back to Princeton with me for the start of my second year of seminary. One might expect that a school designed to prepare future ministers to deal with life's difficulties would be the ideal place to find healing and solace, but I quickly realized that almost the opposite was true. The Princeton Seminary I returned to had little regard for anything that might get in the way of academic excellence, my peers seemingly only concerned with the markers of their own success that would land them a great job. It was an environment with very little heart. There was little place for someone who was undone by the trauma of such violation. And the upbeat, cheery midwestern seminarian, the young woman who used to sit in the front row of every class asking many questions, was now in the back row, staring out the window, wishing she could be any place else.

I clearly was in what we'd now recognize as post-traumatic stress. I couldn't focus on my work. I feared being alone. I was having violent dreams, waking in a cold sweat thinking the rapist was in my dorm room. I was a mess. The rape experience was unwelcome but the aftermath, with its insistent personal undoing, was almost equally devastating. I didn't know who to go to with the questions, large and small, that had so suddenly disrupted my faith and comfort.

Though not always nursing traumas with the devastating impact of a rape, a handful of students arrived at my door during my early days at Macalester with many questions and concerns. I was delighted to spend time in conversation with them. But I also recognized that, even for someone who desperately wishes to talk about what they're going through, it is sometimes simply too daunting to make an appointment with a chaplain or a counselor. The institution sends out the message that its members can handle anything. And though the stigma of mental health challenges has changed a lot over the past decades, it is still difficult for many students to seek out the support that the institution offers. As glad as I was to spend time with those who made it into my office, I knew that there were many more with needs as great who I never got a chance to meet. I wanted to be available to them as well. It was this impulse that gave my Catholic colleague and me the idea of going somewhat public with our willingness to listen, host questions, and offer a listening ear.

We hit upon the idea the second fall I was Macalester. It came about one afternoon when we were joking about my name, Lucy, and the fact that the creator of the *Peanuts* comic strip, Charles Schultz, was from St. Paul, Minnesota. We thought it would be great to set up a takeoff on Lucy's famous psychiatrist booth, complete with a cup on the table to receive a nickel contribution for five minutes of conversation. We figured it was just offbeat and nerdy enough that it might be a disarming way to help students get to know us and to elicit some conversation.

We knew students had many informational questions for each other: "Where do you buy books?" "Who is your roommate?" "Where are you from?" "What is your major?" We also heard them ask questions that were a little riskier: "Who was that guy you were walking with?" "How did you do on your paper?" "Are you feeling okay?" "Are you looking forward to going home for break?" Roc and I also suspected there were many questions that roamed around in the heads of young adults (and older adults as well) that never got asked: "What happens after we die?" "Why is there suffering in the world?" "I am worried about my friend who is drinking every night. What can I do?" "Will I ever find an intimate relationship?" "I am lonely. How do I make friends?" These were the kind of questions we heard behind the closed doors of our offices, but which we wanted to invite from others who would never think to seek us out on their own.

So we set up a table in the college snack bar with a sign on it, "LIFE'S BIG QUESTIONS ENTERTAINED HERE." Two chaplains on one side of the table, two empty chairs on the other, plus a cup to receive the nickel (a gimmick, but one that somehow made it clear our invitation was partly tongue in cheek). The first several weeks we sat at the table through the lunch rush, only students who knew us in other contexts stopped to greet us.

Then, on the fourth week, we were eating our lunch and chatting with a colleague who worked in the building when two women students walked past. I didn't know them, but one nodded at me. I smiled over my colleague's shoulder. The women both headed to the mailroom but then a few minutes later approached the table. The one who had nodded came toward me and asked if they could make a time to talk. Our colleague immediately excused himself and Roc and I invited the women to sit down.

"So, do we pay two nickels or one, if we have the same question?" the second woman asked. Roc and I looked at each other. Students always come up with angles we don't anticipate.

"One will be fine, but if you wind up needing more time, you may need another nickel," I said with a wink.

We introduced ourselves, as did they. Jenna was a sophomore from California, and Maggie a sophomore from Missouri.

"So, tell us what your question is," Roc said.

Maggie started in. "How do you choose a major? We have to decide next week and don't know what we want to major in."

"Did you talk with your advisors?" we queried.

"Yes, but their advice is too intimidating." I sensed that there was some other, more pressing question below the surface of this topic.

Suddenly Jenna came out with it. "If I want to leave Macalester, do you think I'd be a failure?"

Maggie chimed in, "She's been wanting to go home for a year but is afraid everyone will think she failed."

Roc and I looked at each other. He responded, "Jenna, who ever said there is one way to live your life? What is your heart telling you? Is there something drawing you home?"

Jenna's eyes dropped. She shook her head. Maggie draped her arm around her. "Really? Do you really think I could just go home? I am not sure what my family would think of me. But even thinking it is an option makes me feel better."

Five cents in a cup and a connection is made.

Asking. The way to clarify is to begin with a great question. Or as Rainer Maria Rilke says, "Be patient toward all that is unsolved in your heart and try to love the *questions themselves* like locked rooms. . . . Do not now seek the answers, which cannot be given you because you would not be able to live them. And the point is, to live everything. *Live* the questions now. Perhaps you will then gradually, without noticing it, live along some distant day into the answer."[3] That day in the snack bar, what had started as almost a joke—how much insight could anyone really expect for a nickel? —had turned into a moment of release for a young woman who had been struggling alone for months with how to best shape her life going forward. For Roc and me, it reinforced the power of the promise we'd made on our sign—not that we'd *answer* all of "life's big questions," but that we'd *entertain* them. Our job at that desk and as chaplains wasn't always to provide answers—rather, it was to be present and welcoming for their asking.

There are also times, especially in the midst of shipwreck, when the questions we must hold and make room for are even more profound and hard to articulate than Jenna's that day. These are the moments and the questions that shake faith for all of us.

My home phone rang at 2 a.m. on a February night. No call brings good news at that hour. Even before the usually energetic dean of students gave me the details in a whisper, I felt sick with worry.

"Lucy, a student, Brittany Stephens, has been missing for several days. She apparently left a party late on Friday. Her boyfriend thought she went home," he shared. Though Brent, the boyfriend, hadn't heard from her, he had assumed she had gotten there safely. But earlier on Sunday evening, Brittany's mom had called him, saying she'd been trying to reach Brittany for the last day but had gotten no response and was wondering if he knew where she was. As they talked, Brent began to panic. Though he didn't share this with her because he didn't want to worry her any further, he knew that Brittany had left the party pretty drunk and also pretty upset for reasons that were not yet clear. As soon as Brent hung up with Brittany's mom, he called the dean of students to alert him to the situation and to get some help. He told the dean as much as he could, through sobs. Everyone knew that going out alone on an icy Minnesota winter night was dangerous. The police were called.

The word went out and about midnight friends had begun pouring into the dorm where Brittany lived. They were gathering in one of the dorm lounges and the dean wanted me to be there, to listen and simply be supportive of them at this scary time.

"I'll be there in five minutes," I said. Heart in throat, sleep in eyes, I pulled on a pair of jeans and a sweater and decided to drive the three blocks to campus. It was too frigid and dark to walk. In a moment of crisis such as

3. Rilke, *Letters to a Young Poet,* 35.

this, I wonder if I have enough trust, enough faith, enough confidence in the power of God.

I met the dean of students at the residence hall door. Inside, students were sitting on the floor with their fluffy comforters pulled around them. There were about twenty of Brittany's floor-mates and Brent, her boyfriend. I have been with students in many settings but never have I entered a room full of students this silent. They were staring at the floor, holding hands; a few sobs pierced the silence. They were terrified that Brittany was gone.

The dean shared what he knew from the police and family. He assured the students that the college was doing everything it could. He asked if anyone had questions. Silence. He caught my eye and nodded. My turn. I knew they had questions, but maybe not the ones the dean had seemed to be inviting.

I moved from the door and sat down on the floor, at eye level with most of them. I looked around the room—I recognized a few faces. Andy, whose arm was laced around Patricia, was the jokester in every setting where I knew him. At that moment he was glazed over, sallow. Patricia was fumbling with a shredded tissue. I didn't know what to say. I was completely without words. I started there.

Verging on tears myself but knowing the students were grasping for any strand of something resembling hope, I simply started.

"I don't know what to say." My voice broke. "I know we are all scared. Our minds go to the worst possibility. Every time the phone rings we hope. Every person that comes through the door is Brit." I stopped. The first one to let out a sob was Andy. Then Brent doubled over and three others held him. Tears flowed.

That night in the dorm with shredded hearts, eyes cast upon the horizon for even a small sign, we all encountered shipwreck. Even though they were together, the students were castaways on a far shore with few provisions to sustain them. When trouble shows up, when something jars or shatters what is known, you learn what you and others are made of.

When shipwreck happens in the context of an institution, especially one centered around young people like the *in loco parentis* model of American universities, the role of the support staff is to provide an anchor in the form of conversations and resources to those experiencing trauma. That night the institution had entrusted the dean of students and me to be the anchor for distraught students, to hold the fear and try to quiet the rocky seas of that group. Elsewhere, every effort anyone could think of was being mobilized to locate the missing student. That night in the dorm lounge, my contribution was to look into the hearts of students, to listen as they named their trepidation and to hold the collective fear of how we would move forward if she were gone. It was not possible or even helpful for me to offer them false confidence—rather, I tried to invite, validate, and make space for the many unanswerable questions we all felt tossed by that night.

The next day we held a campus meeting to share the news of Brittany's disappearance. Hundreds of students, faculty, and staff came to the chapel. The only fresh and remotely hopeful news was that she had been in touch with a friend from home after she left the party. But no one had heard from her since. Faculty members held students; staff and faculty lingered in the chapel afterwards. The college president spoke reassuring words. I stepped to the pulpit and paused with tears welling. "We are holding Brittany's family in our prayers this day. Hold each other tenderly. This is hard but we cannot lose hope." That was all I could offer, though I was aware that beneath the words I said aloud were other words, spoken to the Source of life and the One who held my hand as I spoke. I silently prayed: "Oh, God. Find us this day in our sorrow and guide us all to peace. If the outcome is tragic, if she is gone, find us in our raging grief. Amen."

As students left the chapel I overheard a group talking. "We can check the shelters in Minneapolis. If she was scared she might have gone there where no one would know her." I was moved by their capacity to keep thinking of how to tap resources when so many other possibilities had already come up short. I heard later that students went to every homeless shelter in the region to see if Brittany had been there. They contacted crisis lines, counselors, hospitals, every agency or resource they could to see if she had contacted them. No word. Faculty took extra time to talk with students, to name what the young adults were afraid to name, to recognize that tragedy interrupts the flow of life even in the academy, and to offer the perspective that at moments like these, the most urgent questions are completely unanswerable. The Macalester community showed up with courage and sorrow.

I wish I could make this a happy ending but it wasn't. As we were to discover a few days later, Brit had ended her life. The college wept, as did God, I believe.

In my work as a college chaplain, moments like this one jar not only the faith of those I work with but reach into the deep fear I have: that life is all folly, "a poor player that struts and frets his hour upon the stage and then is heard no more,"[4] as Shakespeare so powerfully evokes. I would be dishonest if I withheld my own doubts, my own shaken faith, my own big questions.

Rather than shrinking back from the ever-present and pressing question of whether there is a God who acts in any way, let alone small ways in the life of humanity, as a chaplain on a secular campus I realize that honestly facing these questions is itself an act of faith. As I look into faces of incredibly smart young adults who worry that all they are doing is in vain, that their education will lead nowhere, that life is coming to nothing, I feel keenly my responsibility to hold those questions and to try to provide anchors, if not answers, in moments of trauma.

Sharon Daloz Parks's metaphor of "shipwreck" originally comes from theologian H. Richard Niebuhr. He notes that in moments of crisis, faith follows a pattern, moving from shipwreck to the recognition that when one survives, there is pervasive "gladness" that then gives way to "amazement." I think Niebuhr got it exactly right.[5]

It is the role of chaplains and other campus "adults" to witness and hold students through both moments of shipwreck and experiences of gladness and amazement. Often when the dark night subsides, a faint glimmer of light on the horizon gives way to the bold, beaming sunrise in students' lives. Sometimes it happens when I happen to run into a student out on the many walks I take in the college's neighborhood. Out for my daily constitutional, trying to walk off my middle age "gains," I see Justin coming down the walk toward me, out for a run. He sees me, pauses, running in place, and tells me that he is doing a lot better than he was. I see it. The mask-like depression that held back his wonderful smile is gone. The twinkle has returned. And I realize that, as the psalmist tells us, "Weeping may endure for the night, but joy comes in the morning" (Ps 30:5). My work is to keep these dear ones safe, to get them to other professionals who can provide the necessary support of medicine, shelter, therapy. But my work is also to comb the terrain of the human spirit that is remarkably resilient, when it dives deeply into the site of the shipwreck and discovers amazing treasures buried there. Yes, shipwreck has its gifts. And drawing these from the depths is at times my deepest vocation—of holding the person in his or her vulnerability and of recognizing my own vulnerability.

---

4. Shakespeare, *Macbeth,* Act 5, Scene 5.

5. Parks, *Big Questions,* 27–31.

Standing with the community as we grieved Brittany, I realized how many times I have looked into the face of death and how unprepared I felt every time I found myself in this position. *Do I hurry to push the fear of death out of view in a community comprised of 2,000 young adults who assume they will never die? Or is my work to disclose the power of life, to affirm the charging energy of all that says "yes" to this world?* And how can we possibly understand what drove the child who couldn't face life to take her own, or that our own desire to find meaning and purpose is sometimes only met with silence? Sometimes the only response is to simply be there and to have faith that not fearing one's own big questions will empower others to entertain the questions that most trouble them.

In that long-ago summer, I couldn't yet see it this way, but though I was devastated by the attack and deeply shaken by the police officer's response to me, Jack's gentle loving care for me set the possibility way out on a dark horizon, so that my broken heart and broken trust would mend. My own gladness still lay ahead.

—————— CHAPTER 7 ——————

Care for the Soul

A s I PREPARED TO drive back to Princeton in the fall of 1976, it would have been hard for me to imagine another return to campus I would make twenty-five years later to complete a Doctor of Ministry degree. Yet, it would not have surprised me to encounter a literal dark night that would stand so clearly as a metaphor for so much that happened that year and in my work as a chaplain.

I hadn't given much thought to the graduation ceremony itself in the spring of 2001, assuming it would be similar to my first graduation ceremony in 1979, when I received my Master of Divinity degree. Princeton Theological Seminary has a high regard for tradition, only changing things up with much deliberation. As it turned out, this commencement was unique, but for reasons no one could have anticipated.

The ceremony in 2001 was scheduled for the evening because renovations to the Princeton University Chapel had made it unavailable during the day. At the appointed hour, 7:30 p.m., those of us graduating made ready to process. Scaffolding covered the outside of the building and made its way inside, actually blocking a direct passage through the heavy doors, with their ornate etchings. But even with the obstacles, inside the place shimmered. There is nothing quite like a ceremony entering from a dark hallway into the light of a holy space. We were ushered in to the grandeur of organ music sounding through enormous pipes, a line of academic gowns in orange, black, and purple, with velvet and silk academic hoods falling from the shoulders with brilliance. By contrast to commencement ceremonies at Macalester College, where there is a lot of shrieking, hugging, little pomp and a lot of circumstance, here, as the line of graduates made its way forward to be seated there were no spontaneous displays of emotion, just the organ processional. The Seminary president, tall, balding, led the way with a slow, deliberate gait. I felt more like I was at a church service, a stiff one, than a grand celebration of accomplished graduates, and yet joy wafted through the chapel in a sort of Princetonian understated way.

The pecking order of graduates placed me near but not at the front. Ahead of us were the PhD candidates because theirs was the highest academic degree given. Yes, the terminal degree. They had attained the stature of their teachers and would take the mantle of greatness to new heights. We Doctor of Ministry candidates were professionals of note but not ever to be confused with those receiving the PhD.

As we were seated, a hush fell over the crowd, though there was not much to hush. Under ornate lamps showering the room with light, the seminary choir sang a joyful anthem, and we all sang the hymn, "Draw Us In the Spirit's Tether." We listened to the commencement address, that year delivered by Seminary's president. I don't remember anything he said but I do remember my heart leaping into my throat when the time came for the "conferring of degrees," as the program read. We had been instructed to step out into the aisle when the chief academic officer announced, "Will the candidates for the degree Doctor of Ministry please stand?" As our names were called out, one by one, we moved from pew to platform, our left hand grasping the diploma, our right hand shaking the president's hand. As I stood there, I took an extra milli-second to pause and drink in the beauty. To this day, it rests gently in my mind.

I was thrilled that my mother had come from Iowa. My younger brother was gravely ill with cancer and though it was a question up to the last minute whether Mother would be there, she made the trip. I was quite stunned when two Macalester students, twin sisters, tapped me on the shoulder as soon as I sat down, and with camera in hand took a photo that sits on my office desk to this day. In it I am turned around with one of those joyful, silly grins, irreverent and cheeky.

The president pronounced the benediction and with that, a grand organ recessional started up. We once again stood and prepared to exit the chapel.

Because I was one of the first to exit, I saw the doors flying open in the back. And beyond the doors? Pitch black. Not so much as a porch light led us from the ceremony. The sandblasters had unplugged the external lighting system and our university hosts had forgotten to ask them to reattach it. All the lights that were to guide the churchgoers from the chapel had been unplugged due to the renovation and whoever was planning the event, with its atypical hour, simply forgot that the sun sets about 9 p.m.

Within moments, someone's grandma had tumbled down the three steps; a woman with triplets in a stroller tripped and practically flung the babies, diaper bags, and the graduate dad over the threshold, down the steps and onto the ground. Because of the ceremony of it all, no one felt free to forewarn the two hundred or so graduates recessing. The charged excitement of graduation from seminary plunged the graduates into the dark night beyond.

It was not lost on some of us that this is not a bad metaphor for what these seminary degrees prepare us for: stepping into the darkness and finding our way. But none of us thought we'd *literally* have to face the dark night right away. We had to grope our way out the door, find our footing on the steps and then hunt around on the patio to find our family members.

Often I find myself tripping over thresholds from light into uncertain darkness as I work with individuals, families, and the fragile soul of an institution in times of crisis or uncertainty. When the college president approaches me at a board meeting where I am to deliver the invocation and shares with me that a board member's husband has been diagnosed with terminal cancer—"Lucy, please include this in your prayer, but don't be too specific; it will be too hard"—this momentary darkness plunges my soul into uncertainty because I feel caught between the disclosure and the need to quickly revise the prayer that I have so carefully crafted. The question for me is how to hold the community's anxiety and worry with deep respect for privacy and respect.

I step to the podium, in this instance, and looking into the faces of the institutional board members, I see the twinge of worry in their lined faces. The board member whose husband is ill sits in her expensive suit and matching heels, eyes tired with worry. And as I shift from the day-to-day world of student meetings or great discussion groups on interfaith dating into a moment of prayer, I fear tripping and falling into the darkness. I stand before this religiously diverse group of board members, pull the typed-out prayer from my pocket with the handwritten scratches and arrows of revision.

> *Gracious Creator and Life-Giving Hope for this world. On this day*
> *we give thanks for the manifold love and joy that pour into our lives*

each day. For friends and family, for colleagues and counselors, for students and staff, for all that winds its way into the deeper channels of our hearts, we give thanks. There are days when we are in need of support and care; when the world clamors with seething pain; when war rips the heart of a society and the wider world; when efforts toward making peace unravel; we as the human community await the inbreaking of your presence for our day.

There are many on this planet and in this community who face un-certainty in their lives. Hold them tenderly, Most Holy One. Bring healing calm, steady trust, and the holding power of community. AMEN.

I don't know if this is what the president had in mind. I do know that I stand with the board as a fellow traveler through the uncertainty. But I am the one entrusted to speak, who stands between soul's uncertainty and the mystery of life and death for that matter. It is daunting. It is a deep and holy privilege.

On that unexpectedly dark Princeton night in May, no one could possibly have imagined the darkness that everyone in America would feel a few months later, on September 11.

Across the country and across the globe everyone could tell stories of where they were when they heard about the attack on the World Trade Center, the Pentagon, and the plane crashing in Pennsylvania. Everyone had stories of people they knew who lost lives on a plane or in the Twin Towers collapse, how it changed their thinking about safety, travel, or how they thought about God, the problem of evil, people from different faith traditions, or the future itself.

It is one thing to have a personal crisis that places an individual in a vulnerable spot. It is another thing when institutions find themselves lost, unable to deliver assurances of safety and protection for students and the rest of the academic community. Where does the soul of an institution show up and what is the chaplain's role in it? Chaplains stand ready to steady the blows when everything is tossed and tempests roar. But when fear drives the human heart to race out of control, a college campus must also be a place where students' balance can be steadied; where the heart of the campus must hold assurance, peace, arms wide open for an embrace of assurance. How does a chaplain reach out for the institution's soul to help it cross to safety?

We gathered in the chapel at noon on 9/11, just a few hours after the attacks. We assured students the best we could—the president, the dean of students, and myself, all of us shaking in our boots. That day I let my own emotions guide my message to the community. Not unlike the decision to share the rape experience with students, I stated my own fear—how when hearing about the Twin Towers and then the Pentagon and later the plane crash near Pittsburgh, I feared that the known world was coming apart. I stood before that community with tears in my eyes, not only because I could not imagine what this community, many of whom were far from home, but also what the world would do to respond to this development. I said that I feared for their families, knowing that many of them were from the New York and DC metro areas. I remember simply pausing and holding the silence, which, in many ways, was what this terrible tragedy seemed to call for in all its irony. I heard someone's loud sob and arms quickly took wing to hold her. As others began to cry, fear filled that packed chapel, and I noticed Jonnie, a student who I knew was from New York City. She had proudly told me at her orientation the year earlier that her high school was a few blocks from the World Trade Center, an amazing landmark in New York City.

"Yes," I had shared with her, "I had brunch one time by the windows at the World Restaurant at the top of that place. I might have been peering down on your school that morning."

I caught Jonnie briefly after the gathering.

"How are you doing?"

"My family lives very near the Towers and it's the first week of school at my high school." She was quite upset, not only about what was happening in New York but also that the college decided to hold classes as usual. The administration had decided it would be better to hold class, devoting that time to talk about what had happened.

I left the chapel and walked to the Campus Center. Cynthia ran up to me. "Chaplain, I just heard that my two friends doing internships at the World Trade Center are okay. They were off-site doing a project. Whew! I am off to class." She gleefully walked on.

A few minutes later I heard students casually talking about the party they were planning for Friday night . . . business as usual.

On September 12, 2001 I was heading home after having spent a couple of hours that afternoon in our campus center watching the horrible images of fires and haze streaming across every mode of media imaginable. I saw Jack, another student from Manhattan, sitting alone on a campus bench. One look at him told me he hadn't slept. Eyes bloodshot, scruffy whiskers, hair a sight. Dazed and serious, he jumped a little when I spoke to him.

"Jack, I know you have family in New York. Have you heard anything?"

He stood up at that moment, as if courage would expand to his 6'4 frame from the small corner of fear he sat with on that bench.

"I was up all night trying to get through to my family. No cell reception but my aunt in New Jersey finally got a call from my mom. My family is okay. My brother's wife works at the Center. But, can you believe that she had not gone in to work because their dog was sick and she was cleaning up after it? What a moment: vomit saved her life!"

"Thank God, Jack."

But it was not relief that lined his furrowed brow. His eyes grew dim, distant, and kicking a stone with the toe that stuck through a hole in his tennis shoe, he said, "My sister-in-law's father is missing. They can't get through to him. He worked on the forty-fourth floor." We both stared at the stone that rolled down the grey pavement.

Jack looked up and his words echoed Jonnie's, "You know, I just can't believe this college held classes yesterday! How can we just go on with business as usual as if nothing has happened? I went to the vigil for campus and the packed chapel made me think people were really taking this seriously but then just going on with life as if it was just another crisis. . . . I can't believe it. My sister-in-law's father may be gone . . ." Jack let out a sob and slumped over. "Sorry. I am not doing well."

I reached for his arm. He turned toward me, his backpack slipped from his elbow to the ground, and I held his trembling body, draped over my shoulders. He simply held on to me. After a time I felt the ripple of the sobs give way to a short breath expelled from a very large frame. My small frame worked to hold his grief, his deep, deep sadness, and his fear. Slim hope holding boundless grief. He exhaled, stood, picked up his backpack, and brushed the sleeplessness and worry aside for the moment. "Thanks. I guess I'll go to my lab." I stood still for a long moment, watching him wander toward the science building. Broken heart, broken gaze, broken world slung on his back. In the pause, and I don't know if it was a swear or a prayer, I heard the words, "Oh, God."

Jack was right about people going on their way as if nothing happened. Yes, the college had an assembly and of course it offered support for students affected. There were discussions in classes. But Jack and the others saw the tendency to move forward, to rush back into the safety of routine. To hold at bay the fear or worry or vulnerability. I had my own questions that day as well. What is my role as chaplain? Along with other college administrators, I am there to support students. I know that my work is to crawl from my devastation and stand up, looking into the eyes of students like Jack. I often find myself praying, literally allowing words to form in my mind, calling out from the depth of pain and fear to God. "Come, Holy God. Give me strength. Hold this precious child. Hold me. Hold this your trembling world." And in those fragile, vulnerable, tender moments, when I am simply ill-equipped to stand by myself, I know beyond the shadowy doubts that cling to my soul that I am not alone.

That afternoon, I remember walking away with a certainty that Jack and I were not alone. It wasn't a mystical assurance. It was something in the trust that Jack exhibited in his sheer grief. When facing the void of life, the deep pit, he could either resign himself to futility or, as he did, shake his fist at the injustice. He and I found ourselves on holy ground, though we didn't name it that way. A community, local and global, brought face to face with evil. The human community is oddly resilient in its ability to long for something just, hopeful, a sprig of new life arising from the floods of our time. But not too quickly, I must add. Not turning immediately from pain but rather resting long enough to acknowledge it is an important part of hope and healing.

Who wasn't shipwrecked following 9/11? In her use of Niebuhr's metaphor, Sharon Daloz Parks reminds us that when we wash up on a new shore there is loss as well as enlargement. She writes, "The gladness on the other side of shipwreck arises from an embracing, complex kind of knowing that is experienced as a more trustworthy understanding of reality in both its beauty and its terror."[1] Throughout the ages the human community has tried to come to terms with the problem of evil in the world. Many persons' individual lives are exempt, somehow, from trauma. Nevertheless, the contingency of life, with the reality that in the end we all die, presses upon the human community.

The fatal flaw of the human condition is out of view for many young adults. Chaplains who work with young people are hard-pressed to convince

---

1. Parks, *Big Questions*, 30.

this population that they won't live forever. And yet, as someone who in my young adult years was brought quite starkly into the presence of my own potential annihilation, I recognize those who arrive at college with a history of loss, or moments of reckoning with the power of hurt at the hands of another, or the inner angst that often shows up as depression or anxiety. I know this territory well.

When something as monumental and soul-jarring as 9/11 happens it is quite usual for other traumatic events that one has experienced to enter or reenter the psyche, the spirit, and bring one face to face with emotional wreckage once thought over and gone.

All year, I had students and faculty members arrive at my door with worries that were not present prior to that fateful day. One student suffered from the nightmares and anxiety that plagued many people across the country; another felt the overwhelming desire to go home to be near family; one faculty member struggled with the combined effects of worrying about her child who was away at college and the stress of missing several project deadlines because she simply couldn't concentrate. I could not remove the very real, very dark source of their stress, but I could offer a steady, unjudging presence, a compassionate heart and the companionship of someone who knew what it was like to find my way through a very dark, scary, upsetting time in my own life.

About a week after the rape, I left Seattle to head back to Princeton for the fall semester. My friend, Ellen, who had been in Oregon working as a hospital chaplain intern, had planned all summer to "road trip" back to New Jersey with me, but now I was especially glad to have her along. The week-long trip held hours of worry and fear, but mostly silence. I told Ellen what had happened. She was deeply sensitive and caring, offering as much space as she did loving support.

But when the nightmares began a few weeks after I got back to Princeton Seminary, I didn't know what to do or where to turn. I felt ashamed. I thought I needed to deal with it alone.

Almost every hour I found myself terrified, imagining that the footsteps behind me were a rapist. Sitting in a library carrel alone, I feared that someone would come up behind me and attack me. Many nights I woke up panicked that the rapist was in the room. I just wanted to replay my life and delete that episode. But it couldn't be done.

I didn't know at the time about Post Traumatic Stress Disorder. When I later came across its definition: "A debilitating mental disorder that follows experiencing or witnessing an extremely traumatic, tragic or terrifying event. People with PTSD usually have persistent frightening thoughts and memories of their ordeal and feel emotionally numb, especially with people they were once close to."[2] I recognized immediately exactly what I had experienced in the aftermath of the rape. I was living with an unwelcome trauma that I had no capacity to understand.

I needed the care of an adult mentor, an adult initiator, who would take me through the rough patches and offer the possibility of an enlarged trust that could incorporate the fear, mistrust, violence, undoing. When one is plunged into the darkness of trauma, having the holding love of an adult such as a chaplain goes a long way in making one's way to the glimmers of the dawn. As I think back on the fall semester, 1976, I don't know if I would be alive today, had it not been for that aeminary professor/chaplain who held the door open to the possibility that God meets us at the threshold of pain, fear, and violence.

Over dinner one night, a friend whom I had gotten to know when we were in a class on human development the year before listened to me describe a bit about my struggle and suggested that I make an appointment with our former professor, Dr. Jim Loder, to talk. By this time I was in a deep crisis, or deep shit as our students would say. My grades were plummeting. I couldn't concentrate, but I also didn't care about seminary, my work, my life, or God for that matter. I had nothing to lose. I made the appointment.

Dr. Loder agreed to meet with me. He was very clear with me, though, that our work would be grounded in the Holy Spirit's guidance. I nodded when he said that, though honestly, I had no idea what he meant. He was a kind, brilliant, sensitive man. I was a wrecked, fearful, sorry soul who was in crisis. Each week I entered his office, exhausted from a string of sleepless nights, raw emotions, and fear that I'd never shake what felt like a nightmare I couldn't wake up from. I brought questions much like those of the students who came to me after 9/11: *Will I ever be able to trust the world again? Will I be able to trust God? Who is there to support me? To listen? Who understands when all you've understood about life comes unstuck?* Through conversation, he helped me realize that, rather than restrain the fear, the invitation is to welcome the fear. "Because," Dr. Loder reminded me, quoting

2. http://psychcentral.com/disorders/ptsd/.

1 John 4:18, "there is no fear in love. Perfect love casts out fear." He also suggested the possibility that the dreams I was having might actually be a source of healing.

What was surprising about my time with Dr. Loder was that he was so confident in the healing power of God that he never papered over the most upsetting dynamics that were arising from confronting what I might now call the demons of fear. I also learned from him that acknowledging the most difficult aspects of the human psyche, the human soul, actually reorients us to our true self. We run away from the source of deep healing when we try to make everything better before its time. The counter-move of intensifying the pain, going to the depth of it, actually engenders trust because I was able to know that all of the secrets had "secreted," as Dr. Loder often said. And what are the secrets? That we don't believe we are worthy of love, but that we are loved beyond our own belief. And that we think we have to earn God's favor when we are already loved, so very loved, by God. These were but a few of the treasures I received from this remarkable man. And these are gems that I, in my work as a chaplain, endeavor now to hold before my community. But at the time, these insights were slow in coming to me.

I couldn't have made it through that year without Dr. Loder's patient care. But by spring, it was clear to me that I needed a break from my studies to further collect myself. I decided to take a year off.

Just as I was making this decision, out of the blue I received a phone call from a pastor back in Washington State who was looking for a seminarian to intern in his Baptist church. Though the prospect of going back to the Seattle area was challenging and the thought of working in a church even more challenging, I needed a break from seminary. I was quite lost. For me, it was another moment of groping in the darkness. I had no idea what the year ahead would bring.

CHAPTER 8

Thresholds that Support

Mentoring Young Spirits

I GOT THE INTERNSHIP. As I drove back across the country to Seattle, I thought of the last time I'd traveled this same route, a year before. I could hardly remember who that optimistic, enthusiastic girl had been. What was I doing going back? I felt completely clueless about my personal and professional direction at this stage of my life. But the words my college chaplain had spoken to me as I ventured from Sioux Falls to Princeton a few years earlier still made sense.

"Lucy, just go," he had said. Now as I looked down the road toward Seattle from New Jersey, the word that seemed to be calling from there was, "Just come back, Lucy. Trust that my joy will be made complete in you."

I had a couple of friends in the Northwest, including a close seminary friend who had graduated and taken a position in a church near Seattle. I also wanted to stay connected with my Pastor friend Jack and his wife, Barbara Wilson, with whom I had remained close after the trauma of the summer. They were evolving into deep and caring guides for me—among the first and most important mentors of my young life.

Throughout the following year I leaned heavily on Jack and Barbara's friendship and support. They were always there for a quick phone chat; they had a wonderful swimming pool I could swim in on warm summer days; if I needed a night away from my internship, the guest room was ready. Even the very simple but generous meals, home cooked meat-and-potato dinners like my Iowa mom made, filled me with deep gratitude. I felt like

I'd found the godparents I never had. I never felt like I was a burden. They clearly loved having me come. I was becoming family.

As it turned out, I ended up needing their support even more than I could have foreseen when I first decided to return to Washington. Shortly after I arrived in the small town where I was hired to be the intern, I received a call from the Edmonds police stating that they had apprehended someone who fit the description of my rapist. They asked that I come to the police station and identify him in a lineup. If I had been at Princeton, as planned, they likely would never have called me and I certainly wouldn't have had to face the decision to put myself once again in the presence of the man who had so disrupted my life and sense of self for the last year.

I knew I couldn't revisit that police station by myself, so I asked Jack to go with me. It was a tremendous source of comfort to me that I knew even before asking that he would not refuse. Even without his saying anything, I was reassured by his calm, comforting presence as we made our way to the police station and towards the room where officers accompanied me to a kind of sound-proof booth with one-way glass. If I was going to have to confront once again the man who had raped me, at least this time I wouldn't be alone.

Five men, all with shackles, were led into the adjacent room by two guards. I was to identify if any of them was the man who raped me. Indeed, he was one of them. Seeing the face that had haunted me steadily for so many months again in the flesh and only a few yards away was very unsettling. I knew he couldn't see me through the mirror and would never know that I had finally disobeyed his order not to go to the police, but the irrational part of my brain that had kept me fearing for my life was once again reawakened, even after I left the station. I was living alone and the nightmares returned.

If it weren't for the generous, steadying presence of Jack and Barbara, I don't know what might have happened to me that year. I remember several phone calls to them when I was frightened. They were the ones who said I should move out of the house I was living in alone: "Isn't there someone in the church who might have a spare room?" They encouraged me to talk with my supervisor: "You don't need to stay in the house you are in even if the church folks found it for you. If it isn't working, let them know." I did speak with my new supervisor and also the family who had offered the house. The pastor was hesitant but the family who had rented it to me happened to have a friend who needed a house. We also learned that another family in the church had an apartment in the lower level of their home. I moved to a wonderful lake apartment. The nightmares didn't subside but when I woke up I heard the footsteps of a family readying themselves for the day. I was safe.

Jack and Barbara knew how to be mentors to me. They didn't wrest control from me. They actually did the opposite. They provided the steady foundation so I could take steps toward my full adulthood. It is a rare but precious gift to find mentors like this. In her book, *Big Questions, Worthy Dreams,* Sharon Parks says, "The power of mentoring relationships is that they help anchor the vision of the potential self."[1] At a moment when my reawakened trauma was once again calling my sense of self into question, Jack and Barbara helped me direct my vision to the horizon, to the healthy, happy future self that was still within my power to become.

In my professional life, I am a frequent witness to the tremendous power of mentor relationships. One moment stands out in particular.

In the winter of 2002, I attended a conference at a lovely retreat center near San Francisco. The conference, entitled "Life's Work," gathered representatives from six colleges from around the country. For one session, we had divided up into small groups. Mine made its way to the grass and a bench under a five-hundred-year-old oak. In this group were three or four students, two faculty members, a few staff people and a chaplain, me. The group was discussing the question, "How do you live out your vocation?" After introductions, one of the students—a bright, articulate young woman from an East Coast college—launched into her worry about job prospects once she graduated.

"It is one thing to know what I need to do to get through college. I've mastered that 'vocation,'" Sara said. "Read, write, absorb, contribute. But how do I know what kind of work I should be doing once I am out of college?" Sara raised her eyes from a piece of grass she had been weaving between her fingers. Across the circle was a faculty member from a Midwest college. Shaggy white hair brushed the rim of his glasses. His lined face remained serious even as it softened with a knowing, gentle smile. The young woman waited for him to speak.

"I've been a member of the physics faculty for forty years," he started. "When I was a college senior I had no idea what I wanted to do. The world was at war. I had to serve my country. So I spent four years in the military.

---

1. Parks, *Big Questions,* 81.

When I came home, I knew there was a need for researchers and I started graduate school."

All eyes were on him, as he leaned back. Looking up into the branches of the ancient tree, he continued, "I simply wanted to contribute, to do what was most needed. Though I like this idea of being 'called' to something and though I am not so sure if there is such a thing as a Caller, like God or something, I do know that every day I go to my lab or classroom and try to give my students my very best teaching."

It's what Sara said next that makes me think so often of this moment. Looking into the eyes of this very seasoned faculty member with all the openness and trepidation of someone with her whole adulthood still ahead of her, she said softly, "You give me courage, Dr. Jackson. Courage. Thanks."

It took me a few moments to realize that in that moment I had witnessed mentoring—mentoring at its finest. Under the canopy of that ancient tree, he had drawn forth the imagination of that young woman. Worried about all that might stall her life, she had heard in the professor's words and perspective a newly opened way that allowed her to enlarge her horizon.

College or university education in the United States is quite different than university education in other cultures. Rather than training for a job by doing an apprenticeship with someone who has technical skill, the apprenticeship of liberal arts and most university educational settings is for students to seek and secure mentors who serve as adult guarantors, who "help anchor the vision of the potential self."[2] The undergraduate takes four years to navigate a course of study, entering the full-time employment of thinking, challenging, and investigating their assumptions and considering big questions of meaning and purpose. But part of a college education is also found in the pauses along the way. Whether it is the winter recess or summer breaks or time in the quiet of a chaplain's office or reflection groups that provide perspective on internships or service trips, these are times to listen deeply to the heart, the text, the teacher, one's peers. A colleague called these moments the "speed bumps" in the course of what is often the fast-paced life of college students. Reflective opportunities take students into the territory of the human soul where dreams reside. Sometimes the dreams can be spacious and grand. Other times they can be upsetting to others whom students hold dear.

2. Ibid.

Talking to me, a student once described the abundant opportunities that lay before him as terrifying. Looking forward to a career in computer science, he sat with two great job opportunities—one that would land him a handsome salary, stock options in a start-up company, and a move to a great city on the West Coast. The other was at a local non-profit, with a minuscule salary, a great deal of client support but what he described as a mission of "doing good for the world." After a long discussion about the dilemma, he finally confessed that this dilemma had a third component: "Is it wrong to want to hold on to my friends, to stay put, rather than move away for the big-time career? My parents won't get it. They've paid my way here and they want me to succeed." His eye caught mine. His lip quivered and I realized that he was facing the unavoidable fear that shivers around the edges of all good things. I also knew that his work was to step out, to cross the uncertain rapids. I listened to him, trying to ascertain not only the ultimate outcome but how he might take the next step in what would likely be a long series of decisions. "And what do your friends say?"

"Oh, they are all doing what I want to do. They are staying in the Twin Cities next year and becoming adult-like." He chuckled. The air that had gone out of the room now arrived back with his moment of levity.

"Sounds like you'd like to take their course on life as an adult in the Twin Cities."

"Yes, just for a year." Though I was there to watch, to assure, to support, and to let him express out loud a desire he was afraid to admit to other loving adults in his life, this was his journey.

At moments like these, I remember some of my own formative experiences with mentors who offered perspective on the work and decisions that were mine to make.

A few short years after I graduated from seminary I was in my first position in ministry in higher education in Seattle at the University of Washington. The ministry center was located in an old YMCA building half a block from the University.

"It takes time," my colleague, Dave, said one November morning, when a pall of fog hung heavily over the Seattle morning. I had poked my head in his office just as he lit up his cigarette, the second of the day. Dave had been in campus ministry for over twenty years, and had engineered the purchase of the building and held the vision for a deeply ecumenical work.

I had been on the job for less than a year but was feeling uncertain about whether I was having any impact.

"Seems like my efforts are going nowhere," I said. "I've worked on two programs this fall, a feminist theology group and a worship planning group focused on religion and the arts. Not much response. Maybe I'm not cut out for this work."

"You are expecting quick response, Lucy. It takes time in a university. People are busy. Their time is precious. Be patient." He smiled a very gentle smile. I felt the furrow in my brow release.

On that morning and so many like it, I realized that I was, in some ways, still a student. Dave and the other campus ministers who worked at Campus Christian Ministry were my teachers. I was a student of a different ilk than the undergraduates, medical students and PhD candidates who came to our campus ministry center. This was a job and I was now a professional. But nonetheless, part of my task was to absorb and learn what I could from the more experienced campus chaplains I was privileged to call my colleagues.

It was often daunting. Much of the time I felt out of step with my colleagues, who were fifteen to twenty years older than me. The staff was composed of seven professional campus ministers representing ten denominations: Roman Catholic and various Protestant denominations. We were intentionally ecumenical, where one person was sent by and represented several denominations to minister on campus. This model of campus ministry, where a team of specialists is housed in one center, held sway for two decades as an effective way of engaging a generation of institutionally cynical, non-joiner young adults. Issues animated the lives of these ministers and also that of their loyal mentees. Those who did want to join up with a traditional church collegiate group had plenty of options in local congregations. The campus ministry work we were engaged in was funded jointly by five or six mainline Protestant denominations and had as its mission focusing young people who were at the margins of the church and might be more easily engaged in less traditional forms.

I shared one position with my husband, Tom. As young campus pastors in this context Tom and I were hired to bring some "youth" to the enterprise, but after the first wave of welcome, we were on our own to navigate the 35,000-student campus. Our colleagues had their student communities in place. They were social justice ministers with a very ready articulation of a liberal theology. Their phones were ringing constantly with requests for national or international speaking engagements, counseling appointments, invitations to preach or speak in classes. There were books written by them or about them. The ministry center had a distinctive social justice bent focused on feminist theology and anti-war activities such as protesting the proliferation of nuclear weapons in the 1980s Cold War era, an emphasis carried over from a 1960s style of ministry.[3]

Tom and I felt lucky to be able to work closely with people whose careers we so admired, but it was challenging to try to emulate their style of ministry. They were formed by a different set of assumptions. Theirs was the generation that was "speaking truth to power" as the military industrial complex sped through the Cold War era and then tailspun into Vietnam. Now, in 1985, they were putting to bed the 1960s and 1970s, some kicking off the covers, not quite ready to let it sleep, and others taking the commitments they formed then to new heights in protesting the Reagan-era Cold War through anti-nuclear disarmament strategies.

However, Tom and I were of a different generation. Though these campus ministers were clearly ready to mentor us, we did not inhabit their world, their history, their practices. The cultural contrast between us came into sharp relief one wintry Seattle evening when we found ourselves in a hot tub with a whole flock of colleagues.

We were on a retreat at Whidbey Island, just outside Seattle. It was a rainy weekend. The group had met all day, discussing the looming threat of cutting positions in the face of dwindling resources. Tom and I were the last hired and we knew our fate was certain: if cuts came, we'd be the first fired. The day's conversation had been intense for everyone, but especially so for us. Now, we had eaten dinner and were ready for a break. We had heard what a wonderful experience it was to soak in the hot tub as a cool Pacific Northwest rain fell gently. This was our chance! We had gotten our son, Christopher, fourteen months old, down for the night and we were ready to join the others.

We were getting out our bathing suits when it occurred to me that the hot tub dress code had not been discussed with the others. We realized if we went out in bathing suits and they were nude we would have yet another one of those moments like we'd already experienced before, where the norm was to be open, West Coast cool, hippie, easy, and we were too prudish Midwestern or uptight East Coast.

3. For a further description of this experience, see Forster-Smith, "Musings on My Ministry," 173.

"Tom, go out and check out what they are or aren't wearing."

"You always put me up to this, Lucy. You go."

"Oh, just go out and make up some question you need to know . . . like, 'I'm going to get some wine. Anyone need a refill?'"

"Oh, all right."

Five minutes later, Tom came back to our room and started stripping off his clothes. "Nada. Nothing. Clothing optional," he said.

The circle of eight colleagues in that hot tub had cumulative years of campus ministry experience in excess of 250 years. Each had distinguished him or herself by focusing on a specific programmatic area of work on several state university campuses in the Pacific Northwest. Joe was interested in men's liberation issues; Sara in developing a marriage preparation program that was widening its scope to include gay and lesbian couples; Tim worked at the medical school teaching biomedical ethics; Charles had a powerful ministry of hospitality to students by hosting wonderful meals; Dave ran workshops in life/work design and had worked with Richard Bolles of *What Color Is Your Parachute?* fame.

They were some of the people I admired most in the world, but never before had I felt so out of place in their presence. I wasn't sure which made me feel more uncomfortable: the prospect of sitting naked in a hot tub with eight of my colleagues or the fact that my discomfort reminded me that I was too conservative for the liberals and too liberal for the conservatives. This neither-here-nor-there position applied not only to my modesty but also to my theological assumptions, to some extent. I was raised in the moralistic Baptist tradition, where there were clear rules and regulations such as no drinking or smoking, no dancing or revealing clothes, no premarital sexual activity, etc. I also had grown to question many of these guidelines, believing that the life of faith is less about rules and more about mending the brokenness. I had come to realize that Jesus' ministry was to release the bound-up ones rather than bind them up with the encumbrance of strict rules for rules' sake. But that particular evening I realized just how out of place I felt with the 1960s campus minister crowd.

As Tom and I slid into the hot tub, having worn our robes out to the deck and slipped them off at the last possible second before quickly jumping down into the warm water, the stir of disconnect came full force over me. When we joined them the conversation was about how at one time this would have been the moment the joints would have started to circulate. This itself was no big surprise to me as smoking marijuana was common practice at seminary parties through the 70s (though not one I participated in). The real issue troubling me as I sat in the hot tub was that I feared being exposed. Not the physical kind of exposure—that fear had already been realized—but the exposure that I wasn't one of them. They were accomplished specialists in particular aspects of ministry. I was a generalist not having an area of ministry that I saw myself as an expert in. They were activists, taking their commitments to the streets or shaking up their denominational bodies with radical politics or advising the governance of the university or the government of Washington State on justice concerns. I stood at the sidelines, supporting their activism, studying the issues with students and others, hosting conferences on topics like "Peacemaking," "Feminism and the Bible," "Sexual Violence and Religious Communities." But I was a novice campus minister and I felt inadequate, out of place.

I was uncharacteristically quiet that night, listening and watching just how they described their work. Their brilliance and passion intimidated me. I thought some day I'd discover and grow into my niche, bringing my specialty to the campus. I fantasized that I would have a wonderful student cohort like theirs. But that night as the wine glasses filled and emptied, the rain cooled down our steamy bodies and our little Christopher slept peacefully in the guest cottage, I finally excused myself, sliding up and out of the water, escaping eye contact with my colleagues, pulled on my blue gingham robe, and went to bed.

I wasn't wrong—I *would* never carry out ministry in their way. But I had yet to discover that this group gave me the opportunity to come in contact with a range of understandings about ministry, to test my crazy ideas and ask even crazier questions about my mentors' lives. It was a gift at that stage of my young professional development. And ironically, my freedom to become myself was launched by the powerful realization that I would never be one of them. Their model for ministry and their lives were theirs, not mine. Their mentoring instructed me to find my own way, to take risks, to listen to the culture as well as to my own inner stirring. This was my journey. And they also respected my questioning of their patterns, assumptions and lifestyle. This was mentoring at its richest.

How do we find those who might be ready to step into our lives with grace and fury, seeing in us the abiding potential that is just beneath the surface and completely out of view? Are mentors found or do they find us? It is usually at life transitions that a person is most receptive to and even is seeking a mentor. Entering college, transitioning to the summer after the first year, returning from study abroad, or anticipating graduation are among the major transitions in a college career. But other life transitions—the first serious relationship, a break-up, the loss of a friend or family member to tragedy, a global crisis, a surprise that shifts previously held assumptions—all line up as times when having a mentor, a wise counselor, a soul friend, is particularly important. Sometimes students seek me out, asking if I will be in this role for them. Other times the situation warrants the need. But in any case, how do I detect that my role as mentor is invited?

There are times when a student needs a person to walk them through a rough patch. They call me up or email a request. I may or may not see them again after we meet. But quite often students circle back several times, almost as if they are testing whether I am someone who can stay with them through the challenges as well as the daily routine. They often share more with me as our connection evolves, about family, friends, what worries them, but also what delights them. I might walk by them on campus or go to a soccer game or volleyball tournament and they catch my eye. And the next time they just come by to see if I am in the office they tell me how glad they were to see me at their event or to run into me. It isn't all that complicated, really, this mentoring role. But it is both choosing and being chosen. I have to believe that there is divine intervention or enlivening involved. It is simply too gratifying to be random!

There are times, of course, when I am the best person to support the person in front of me and at other times I am not. Sitting with a student whose world revolves around fact, theory, certainty, absolutes, is hard for me. I venture into a conversation with him or her but as I put my ideas before them, or listen intently and find myself quieted, I realize that this young person needs someone else. I can't track with them. I admit my inadequacy, not apologizing but simply referring them to someone else who might be more helpful. On the other hand, there are students and others who come to me and in an instant we are off and running in our conversation. I offer a thought and they pick it up: "Have you read any of Paul Ricoeur's work?"

"No, I haven't heard of him."

"His concept of the second naiveté is one you might want to explore as you step into your faith questions."

"Tell me about it . . ."

As I watched the interaction between the professor and Sara across the circle seated on the grass, and as I listened to the bright, capable young man in my office choosing between two career paths, I witnessed the delicate beginnings of a mentor relationship. For those of us in the mentor role, it isn't our work to hold their hands as they make their way across a stretch of life's treacherous coursing. As a matter of fact it would be an insult to their full potential if we did. We give instruction for the task: *Watch the currents, wear the right skid-proof shoes, step and steady yourself, and make sure to hold your breath if you happen to hit a drop-off!* As a mentor I have watched others make their way across rapids and nearly drown. I have also observed them step gingerly and find their way to far shores. Instruction or coaching is important but it doesn't guarantee the safe passage. And if the mentee gets in over her head, if she slips under undetected, and doesn't surface, as a mentor I need to have the presence of mind and also be in top form to wade in and pull her out before she drowns. I do this with students. I also have done this with my own children.

I am convinced that it is only because I had such amazing mentors myself that I am even in small measure able to give this gift to those who come my way.

One spring evening, I was having dinner at the Wilsons' condominium in Edmonds. I hadn't seen them for a few weeks. They were asking me about my year. Though I appreciated the experience of working in the Baptist congregation, I realized I was carrying a lot of baggage both from the rape experience and also from my moralistic upbringing in the Baptist church. I felt confined by the rules and regulations I encountered in that church.

I shared with Jack and Barbara that I was not feeling excited about ministry in the Baptist church. I had run aground with some of the youths' parents over a unit on sexual behavior. They were rigidly moralistic in their approach with their teenagers, not realizing that many of the kids were already sexually active. They saw me as the liberal from the fancy East Coast seminary and were critical of my desire for young people to know not only the rules about sexual activity but to consider how the rules came to be and how they might be applied to specific situations. Ethical and moral development was my interest but my version of it did not seem to be the same as the parents of the teens I was working with.

Jack listened to my complaint and then teased me gently: "Sounds like you may be looking for a new denomination. You know the Presbies would love to have you if you ever need a new church home."

It was another one of those moments. Just as on that starry long-ago night on my family's front porch and on the otherwise normal morning in the campus coffee shop when my undergraduate chaplain drew my attention to a Dylan lyric, something like an electric shock went through me. I knew with total certainty that I needed to make the change and to become a Presbyterian.

"So, if I were going to become Presbyterian," I ventured, "what would be involved?" And with a look of such joy, such surprise and a large measure of grace, Jack and Barbara swooped me up in the loving embrace of a faith community. They talked through the process and I started right away.

Within a few months I had joined Jack's congregation. A new life of faith had begun. I had left Princeton not knowing how the year would evolve, and now as I prepared to return, I realized I had shaved off most of the familiar territory of my life and was standing on the cusp of a very new adventure—a new denomination, a new vocation, a new year—and the very clear sense that I had stepped over some threshold into adulthood.

The irony was not lost on any of us that in joining Jack and Barbara's congregation, I was joining the very church where I had been raped. Instead of fleeing the site of the event that had so shattered my innocence, I had evidently decided to reclaim it as a place of healing and possibility. I would never have been able to make that important choice for myself without the caring, graceful support of my mentors.

The fall of 1978, I drove back east across the desert of central Washington, over the mountains of western Montana, the plains of Nebraska, through Iowa and on to Princeton. That drive once again emerged as a pilgrimage. All that I could have said "no" to in my life had in fact begun to emerge as a powerful "yes" through the remarkable love of my newfound Christian community. I was heading on toward the unknown future, a destination that was less a place on the map and more a grand horizon that simply called me to trust. Once again I could experience excitement at the idea that my future held surprises for me that I could not foresee. God had not abandoned me. And not only that—I sensed that I had much to offer to the world's great needs.

CHAPTER 9

Thresholds at the Margin

The Maverick

THE ENERGY I FELT returning to seminary after my year in Seattle stayed with me through the following months. The depression I'd suffered in my last semesters on campus had been replaced by a politically charged anger. As a rape survivor, I was radicalized not only to my own vulnerability to rape, but also to a culture that practiced violation and violence through power, privilege and dominance, especially toward women. I saw male dominance in the wider culture, keeping women subservient, silent, economically compromised, unable make choices about their bodies. I became aware that many of these cultural realities stemmed from religious convictions, many of which came about through a particular way of reading the Bible. I couldn't escape the laden symbolism of having been raped in a church, a place where the patriarchy has held sway for centuries and where the triune God is Father, Son and Holy Spirit, all of whom are referred to as male. Indeed, the Greek word for Spirit is actually neutral and the Hebrew word for Spirit is feminine, but few realize it, and fewer still ever bother to change the pronoun. In a rather unexpected way it was the frustration with these ideas and my own energy to redress them that was a source of healing and grace in the context of the seminary.

It's possible that this political awakening would have occurred in any era as a natural part of my healing process, but as it happened, the year I was raped was just about the time feminist liberation theology was buzzing through theological education. Around the time I returned to Princeton a newly minted Presbyterian, the Presbyterian Church's Committee on Women and the Church started centering much of its work on women's access to leadership in the church and also on developing inclusive language about God and humans. It was an exciting and complicated time to be a young, female seminarian.

At Princeton, the class I had entered with in 1975 was about one-third female, the largest number of women in the history of the seminary. Though the institution was clearly trying to change with the times by admitting so many women (some cynically thought it was our tuition that was most welcome), the seminary made very few changes beyond taking the urinals out of what had now become the women's restrooms. The walls erected (pun intended) by white male privilege were everywhere.

In the weekly chapel services, the language about God and humans was exclusively male. In the classroom, when women began to ask about the gendered God and the assumption that the term *man* included women too, the mostly male professors dismissed the critique. "*Humanity* is a better translation actually," one biblical scholar told us, "but you have to understand that these are ancient texts and that world was patriarchal. Women simply were not included in much public life." This same professor, who had a remarkable facility with ancient languages, once went on another long-winded digression to defend male-centric interpretations of the text. We were considering the passage from Isaiah where God is compared to a mother who draws her children like a hen to her breast. With a tone so defensive it was clearly not an emotionally neutral lecture, he pulled out his lexicon of Hebrew and proved to us that the term "like" is absolutely not intended to mean that God *is* a mother. We were apparently to overlook the gender implications of metaphorical language in *this* image, but not elsewhere where it didn't upset the common conception of God as male.

The seething anger that crept into his exegetical review freaked my seminary peers and me out. Was this an example of the "open inquiry" the seminary prided itself on? It seemed that this professor was running scared. He was the professor so he had the final word: there is a reason we refer to God as Father—it is biblical. I was in the thick of these discussions in and out of seminary. The issues of language and inclusion didn't feel theoretical to me. The rape had not only brought me face to face with the injustices and vulnerabilities of being a woman but it had also raised multiple theological questions. It was not only my own survival and inclusion that was at stake but a theological tug of war that was raging around me. Especially now, in my last years of seminary, coming to some sort of resolution on them felt vital to the decision whether to proceed toward becoming an ordained minister. I also was discovering an inner strength that made me unafraid to ask the hard theological questions.

At that time, all of us had been raised in religious traditions that spoke of God exclusively as male but now that assumption began to seem to many of us as tied to larger questions of male power and dominance. Once we began to question the assumption that men should naturally hold more power because they more closely resembled a male God, we began to question the related implication: was the concept of an exclusively male God itself just a construct designed to support and affirm a male dominated hierarchy? If women wanted to share in some of the power historically denied us, would that mean utterly rethinking the God of our childhoods?

Political and theological issues aside, I was already grappling with the problems of reexamining my lifelong image of God. Since childhood I had relied upon a basic assumption—God is a loving Father and a father's role is to protect us from all harm. As I began to rethink my conception of God, this became a huge problem for me. Where was Father God when I was raped? Why didn't he protect me? And even more poignant, if a church is the house of God, then, how could the owner of the house let one of his own have something as awful as a rape happen under his watch? Where was God then? Where is God now? In light of what had happened, who or what was I to understand as God?

I sought answers to these personally and intellectually troubling questions, but in the absence of satisfying responses from my professors, my frustration grew.

However, it may not come as a surprise to anyone who has experienced a very difficult, jarring and spiritually upending experience that anger often functions as a mobilizing instead of debilitating force. In my case, anger at the rapist, at the reality that women (and men) are vulnerable to rape, that there is violence and violation on the globe, brought perspective and clarity to me as I considered issues of justice. My anger fueled a contrarian perspective that led me to deeply consider issues I might otherwise have ignored, but it took me a while to figure out how to use this perspective constructively. It was a lesson I learned the hard way.

The summer after I completed my year-off internship in a Seattle suburb, I interned as a hospital chaplain. I loved the engagement with patients, most of whom welcomed a compassionate chaplain who was there to listen and care for them. The clinical pastoral education program provides an opportunity to hone pastoral skill and also gives interns the opportunity to reflect deeply on personal dynamics that support our work and also those that get in the way of effective ministry.

My issues with male authority got me in trouble on several occasions, mostly with physicians. I would question the doctors if I thought they were talking down to patients or their families. I would step into places I should not have been like doctor's lounges and nurse's stations, sometimes by mistake, but at times because I didn't believe in the hospital hierarchies that had the doctors in the privileged role and almost everyone else there answering to them. I thought the moral high ground was a concept that carried the day, no matter the context. But one afternoon I learned the importance of treading lightly while still keeping sight of the moral issues.

I was walking down a corridor when I overheard two attending physicians berating a medical student to the point that she ran for a restroom in tears. When I followed her into the ladies' room, I found her in a state of such distress that she threw up. After spending a few minutes trying to comfort her, my righteous indignation took over. I decided to confront the doctors. When I found them still in the hallway, I demanded to know why they needed to treat another person that way. In my view, I had witnessed a simple case of bullying by powerful men over a lower status woman. By bringing their misdeeds to their attention, I thought, they might be shamed into realizing the cruelty of their actions. Or, at the very least, a fellow woman would not have undergone humiliation at the hands of men without someone else sticking up for her. The doctors' response to me was quite curt. They basically listened for a few moments and then started checking the charts they were carrying, turned and walked away.

A few hours later, my chaplain supervisor pulled me into his office. "I hear you had a conversation with Drs. Rider and Young," he said.

"Yes," I responded. I was still feeling the emotions of the earlier scene, but I could tell from his tone that there was more to come.

The chaplain supervisor was an exceptionally kind and gentle man. But with a force that was uncharacteristic for him, he said, "Lucy, your instincts are fine but your maverick ways must go. You have to respect the physician culture here. You can't disrespect their years of experience and their expertise. Sometimes being a maverick gets you in trouble." I could have gotten defensive but I listened to him. My ears began to burn; I was worried I might be dismissed from the program. I was not. But his words helped me understand that I had not understood the whole picture before reacting. In an institution like a hospital, there is a clear authority system in place, a necessary procedural protocol that keeps patients safe and safeguards against human error. While I might have been right to hear gendered overtones in the doctors' treatment of the student, it was not productive to go charging at them, full of accusations.

As I walked away from my conversation with my supervisor that word *maverick* rang in my ears. I think it was the first time I had ever heard the term. After I ate crow and apologized to the two doctors for overstepping my role, I went to the dictionary in the medical library and looked it up.

The term is associated with Samuel A. Maverick, a late-nineteenth century Texas rancher, who, for whatever reason, did not brand his calves, a fact that no doubt wreaked havoc on the unfenced South and West. This term has evolved in our time to identify someone who is independent and who doesn't go along with the status quo, and who may be considered defiant or simply as one bucking the system.

I learned that being a maverick is challenging and a challenge in certain contexts. But as it turned out, the hospital chaplain advisor was only the first person in my career to call me a maverick. When faculty, supervisors and even friends have described me with that term, there is sometimes an implication that being a maverick is a grave character flaw—but at other times, there's a measure of admiration associated with the term. After all, many new ideas and much culture change arise from mavericks. Over the years, I have discovered that the maverick spirit when judiciously applied can awaken new insight, position one to stand up for the weak, and elicit an unquenchable thirst for justice. It can be a powerful position from which to practice chaplaincy.

In the 1960s and 70s chaplains on campuses often were the ones who "spoke truth to power." They were seen as the conscience of the campus, calling out practices that served to disempower or disenfranchise those with little or no power. Institutions would listen to their voices, watch as they marched for racial, sexual, economic equity, and would understand if they ended up in jail for civil disobedience. The prophet-chaplain had its day.[1] Though today, the voice of chaplains shows up differently on campus, the chaplain often brings both measured insight and also what I like to think of as a maverick spirit.

1. For more on this subject, see Oliver, "In Coffin's Pulpit."

The match of campus and chaplain shows up in humor, heat, and heartache. But the chaplain maverick is someone who carries in her spirit the defiant "no" to all that will undo her; one who stands up with voice shaking and claims uncharted territory, even at the risk of being misunderstood. And even if she is so sure she is right and later discovers she isn't, she continues on with spiritual fortitude, licking wounds and stepping out boldly toward the horizon.

Institutions in general do not welcome mavericks, but I am convinced that there are times when chaplains, faculty, students and others, need to speak out against anything that hurts another person or group of people. Sometimes, stepping over borders or crashing through the fenced-off territory of the campus or of the soul can sometimes be important work for the maverick chaplain.

When the message board on a student's dorm-room door is violated by a racial slur or when a swastika is painted on the door of the Hebrew House, or when a student is assaulted walking from the library to his house a block off campus, and then the steaming anger arrives in response, appropriately, I see the same maverick spirit in others that I feel in myself. I see the power of the maverick when conversations in faculty meetings get bogged down and a creative, brave, challenging professor names the issue or the dynamic that has driven the meeting off course. Most often, there is a twinkle in her or his eye, a knowing that is much more powerful than simply the ability to call up facts and data.

I associate the idea of the maverick with the bravery it takes to let an inner sense of rightness guide one's way into the unknown. It's this spirit I find myself drawing on often in my work. When I watch tears well in a faculty member's eyes after she hears of a college alumnus drowning or when a colleague receives a bad diagnosis from a doctor, I experience the maverick drive toward compassion. My work as chaplain is not about making these distresses all better by papering over hurt, anguish, and upset. When I find myself shaking in my boots, wondering if I will be able to say anything that will help, realizing that I may not be fluent in the emotional, spiritual or cultural language of this new country I venture into, I think I know the world of the maverick. The unbranded nature of spiritual life is one that works well in the often uncharted world of a campus.

Indeed, the very role of higher education is one of challenging students to enlarge perspectives; in doing so, they disrupt the categories they arrive with at college. Anyone who's ever sat around a Thanksgiving table with a liberal arts sophomore can appreciate how this disruption manifests itself in newly formed positions (as well as the aptness of "wise fool" as a description of this particular moment of educational development). But the intellectually rich academic environment must allow for the sophomoric spirit, and actually will encourage it. I find that places like Macalester College with a history of student activism, intellectual edginess, global reach, are often seen as maverick in a culture that wants to have things settled, controlled, predictable.

In retrospect, it was that first realization in the office of my hospital chaplain supervisor that led me to think about how the chaplain must navigate both spiritual and secular institutions and to find her own way, boldly, without borders, through its many complications. Indeed, as a student at a seminary where new ideas were confronting thousand-year assumptions about what comprises the canon of biblical, theological, social, and historical ideas, I was experiencing a culture shift that would later serve me well as a college chaplain. Through seminary, I assumed that the path ahead for me was that I would be an intellectual, someone who stood on the outside of culture and religion and critiqued it. I thought I'd do a PhD and teach either feminist theology or some aspect of theology and the arts. As a radicalized feminist, my theological viewpoint was unbridled. As a musician, poet, and lover of words, the connection between Spirit and art pricked my imagination. Both of these academic areas led me to the creative, imaginative edges. I knew I wanted to find a way forward that would allow me to question and embrace at the same time. I was at a crossroads, a senior seminary student trying to discern the ideal context for the maverick spirit that the hospital chaplain supervisor had only recently named in me but that I had known was there all my life.

It was about that point that I made my way to Rutgers University, about twenty-five miles from Princeton, where I had been a student intern my first year of seminary. It had been almost three years since I'd seen my former supervisor, Hadley Harper. So much had happened over those years. As I entered the house-turned-office, a kind student secretary greeted me. I told him I had an appointment with Rev. Harper. "He is expecting you," the student said.

I started to make my way up to what I knew as Hadley's office but student directed me down the hall on the first floor instead. Hadley was sitting in his new office. He took both of my hands in his, as if I was a long lost daughter. As we discussed old times I noticed that he was thinner and looked tired.

"Are you still involved with the Fuckorama?" I asked. It was a sex-desensitization workshop that he had begun years before that was a requirement for medical students, encouraged by the law school and attended heavily by seminarians and social workers. It was very important for these aspiring professionals to be familiar with the range of sexual experiences their patients, clients, and parishioners might disclose. Rather than being openly shocked or overwhelmed by these, medical students or ministry candidates would, through viewing hours of sexually explicit movies, learn to manage their responses. I thought this was a very daring, maverick program for campus ministry to host, launch, or offer. He replied that the medical school at the university had taken it over, adding that he was having some health issues and was planning to retire.

Hadley had been a campus minister for his entire career. While working with him during my first year of seminary, I noted that current students and many young and middle-aged adults would stop by his office for appointments. I discovered that these were alumni of Rutgers who had gone on to do amazing things. He always had his door open to them. He had a ready handshake, a characteristic wink, and an abundance of love for his work and for these former students. But I also noted that those who came for visits were very unique individuals: women and men, black, Asian, white, Hispanic. Some were hippies, some were Vietnam vets in fatigues, some were top-drawer lawyers in three-piece suits, some donned clergy collars. Clearly, Hadley touched many lives. Truly, he was deeply respected and loved by so many people. Both his work and also his reach fascinated me.

That day we talked about my time at Rutgers, laughing about the fact that I really only had two or three students who I connected with that year. "It didn't matter, Lucy. If you touch one student deeply, that works. We aren't here to woo the masses, we are here to serve God," he said. I sat in silence, looking into his kind, seasoned eyes, lined with years of remarkable vision, gentle insight, caring concern. He asked me about my plans for the future. "I am thinking of campus ministry," I heard myself tell him. A flush crossed his face and with his kindly grandfather's warning he said, "Funding is diminishing or I would encourage you to think of applying for a post here. But, Lucy, don't let that discourage you. You have what it takes."

We went on with the cordialities and I left that afternoon with deep gratitude for the gracious life of maverick saints like Hadley, who loved the university, who never spent an hour worrying about whether they were successful, but only whether they were faithful. He didn't use the word *maverick* that day and neither did I, but I learned from him a lesson that I carry to this day: to be a professional requires a fortitude that allows not only for mighty successes—rooms crowded with adoring students, congregations hanging on every word that proceeds from your mouth, being needed, wanted, desired—but to flourish professionally requires letting go, and even welcoming failure. Holding all these contrary elements together allows one to find a way through the institutional and spiritual unknown, and in Hadley's case, to emerge as a remarkable teacher, affording spiritual, mental, and emotional support to everyone he encountered.

I went home from that visit with a sense of calm and direction I was extremely grateful for. Whether it was the radical changes that had occurred over the last three years during my time as a student or my love of campuses, where intimacy is explored with thought, community, lovers, and friends, I was able to hear again the ringing words of my own undergraduate chaplain: "Lucy, you would make a great college chaplain." I didn't know precisely where the next few years would take me, but I knew at some point in my life I would love to be a campus pastor.

CHAPTER 10

Thresholds of Grace

L IFE TRANSITIONS TAKE STUDENTS and alumni across many thresholds. My role as chaplain puts me squarely at points of major life transition with my constituency. Sometimes these are sad times of loss—whether of hopes and dreams or of life, the deaths of parents or students, by accident or suicide. But more often I work with individuals and couples at transitional moments in their lives that lead to magnificent joy, personal insight, and grace beyond measure. One of those is officiating marriages.

Over the course of my ministry I have stood in front of wedding couples as young as seventeen and as old as eighty. The venues for these occasions have included the Weyerhaeuser Memorial Chapel, many churches large and small, mansions, parks, beaches, an airport landing strip (the couple were both pilots), and a rocky ledge on Lake Superior. I recently officiated at the blessing of the marriage of a same-gender couple in their friend's garden.

Preparing couples for marriage takes on a life of its own, with conversations about the importance of communication, conflict resolution, financial management, sex and intimacy issues, and how families of origin can be a source of support and sometimes a challenging dynamic. Though many religious leaders officiate at weddings, I often find myself standing in front of couples who met in college, who have not grown up in a religious community, or both. I also am quite willing to work with couples who have two different religious traditions such as Roman Catholic and Protestant or Hindu and Christian, or who are only nominally religious themselves but who have family members to whom it is important that a religious figure officiate. Young people's faith traditions often shift or are lost during the college years. When facing the decision about who might prepare them for marriage and then officiate at their wedding, they sometimes find the possibilities limited. They often call or email to inquire whether I do, indeed, officiate at weddings. Once I confirm that I do, they often say something like, "We are of different religious backgrounds" or "We aren't particularly religious. We figured that as the chaplain at Macalester College you encounter all kinds of faith traditions. You seem like a good person to work with us to make our day comfortable and special." They are right that I am open to a range of backgrounds but I also require premarital counseling. We meet three or four times at a minimum to discuss their future life together.

Probably the most challenging couples I work with are those who have recently graduated from college or those who are still in college. Why are these so challenging? I often find myself wondering why they are rushing into such a huge commitment at their tender age. I have watched couples' relationships come apart as they realize they have put so many expectations on their partner to provide support for all their needs. In the premarital counseling sessions with younger couples, I spend time discussing with them how their life will change once they leave the college context, and allow them to talk through how they will navigate the natural transition from college to post-collegiate life and also from their single college years to married post-college years. I strongly encourage them to put into place a great support community. Sometimes this is a religious community but more often it is friends, family, and work communities. But these conversations are not limited to recent-graduate couples. Life in the twenty-first century has many tugs and pulls on relationships. It is a small gift I can give to couples to step out of life's paces and spend time discussing this very important step in their lives. Often the most surprising dynamic in a relationship, one they have not discussed much, is their orientation toward spirituality and religion.

Many couples identify as spiritual but not religious in their orientation toward faith. They bring to their impending marriages religious or spiritual backgrounds that can present challenges to the seemingly simple act of creating the marriage ceremony. If one of the partners is Hindu and the other Buddhist, which tradition should determine the structure and priorities of the ceremony? Or if one person grew up Roman Catholic and her uncle is a priest and the other is the child of a Presbyterian minister, it would seem they would have a ready pool of officiants—why are they coming to me?

As honored as I am to be asked, sometimes a couple's decision to invite a college chaplain to do the honors on their special day indicates a familial or tradition-based tension that I want to be sure they've thought through. Most often, I find, couples who don't feel strongly affiliated with a specific tradition are simply inexperienced in how to put together a wedding ceremony, and unsure of how to navigate its religious or spiritual components. They attend friends' weddings and, like good consumers, pick and choose elements that they like, and discard what they don't like. They want something sacred but most are not quite sure what that means.

One Saturday morning, Jamie and Hal came to my office to plan their wedding ceremony. Both Macalester alumni, they had breezed through the premarital counseling with me. Few issues had shown up for them: *Communication?* Check. *Conflict resolution?* Check. *Family of origin concerns?* Check. *Sexual relationship?* Check. *Spirituality and religious life?* Check. I had gotten the sense from them that they were compatible in their thinking and that they'd put a lot of consideration into what they wanted to prioritize going into their marriage and why they'd come to me as the officiant.

So the morning we sat down to plan the ceremony itself, I was quite stunned when Hal suddenly voiced the adamant position that nothing remotely religious "or spiritual, for that matter!" be included in the ceremony. Up to that point, when we had discussed how they would negotiate religious and spiritual life in their marriage they had both seemed open to its presence in their lives. Neither of them was particularly religious, though they'd grown up with cultural Christianity, celebrating Christmas. They told me that if they had children they would be open to trying out religious communities. It was only when the ceremony content came up that suddenly Hal took a very hard line.

"I know you're a religious figure, Lucy. But being a chaplain at Macalester College—I mean, hardly anyone believes in God here!—I figured you wouldn't care what we have in the ceremony. You'll be cool with anything."

I glanced at Jamie, who was looking down at the ceremony-planning sheet.

She then spoke in an unusually tentative voice. "Hal, we talked about this and I thought we said we'd be willing to have Lucy do one of her great prayers. You never seemed to take offense at them when she'd do them at campus convos or graduation."

"Well, that was the college ceremony. This is our wedding and I really don't want religion of any kind in it."

I took little offense at his comments, actually. I knew he didn't mean to be rude, but in asking me to discard my perspective as a religious figure, he was essentially implying that the very essence of my professional identity and institutional authority was thoroughly expendable. But there's no escaping the facts: I am an ordained minister and it is that very fact that makes it possible for me to marry this couple. If he didn't want to include any hint of spirituality, why ask a religious figure to conduct the ceremony? Why not go to city hall?

And beyond my personal feelings, there were further complications: the Presbyterian Church's *Directory for the Service of God* has clear guidelines about officiating at weddings. As a chaplain I serve a diverse community and certainly stand at the ready to support the range of religious and spiritual commitments of my constituency. But my ordination holds me to standards that I cannot set aside, one of which is that marriage is a sacred act between two people and as a Christian minister I stand at the intersection of my tradition and the couple's. Both for me personally and for my tradition, there was simply no way to separate my religious beliefs and standing from my ability to join two people legally in marriage.

With my mind racing—and facing not only Hal's challenge to me but sensing that he and Jamie were not on the same page—I asked if they had considered having a Justice of the Peace or judge officiate: "Though I am quite happy to work with you on a ceremony that reflects your relationship and your spiritual values, if you want a secular ceremony, it makes sense for you to find a legal representative to officiate."

Hal seemed to be considering this, but then I glanced over at Jamie. She was reaching for the Kleenex box on my coffee table, tears flowing. I knew we were in for a long conversation. "Oh, Lucy, I want you to officiate," Jamie said. "You are so kind, so caring. My mom and dad will love you. Hal, don't you think we can at least have some spirituality in it? I went to a wedding with a judge officiator once. It was so by-the-book. It was really fast. There wasn't that special feeling."

We sat in silence letting Jamie's words fill the room. Hal stared at the floor and then lifted his eyes to meet Jamie's.

I was uncharacteristically nervous in that moment. There are not many times in my work as a chaplain that I'm called on to hold the religion line—in this case, the Presbyterian Christian minister mandates. This was one of them and I was uneasy. Finally, I found the words. "It sounds like this is an important conversation for you two to have without me in the room. I am open to officiating at your ceremony, of course, but as an ordained minister, if you want me to officiate, the ceremony needs to include religious components. I feel it is important to find the right ways to express the spiritual in the ceremony. But I think the two of you need to think about this together. Ultimately, this is not only about the content of your wedding ceremony. This is about your marriage, and how you will live out of deep love and respect for one another."

Jamie was nodding, eyes red, Kleenex torn. Hal's jaw was clenched, though I noticed he had reached for Jamie's hand. I watched them walk out of my office, trusting that they'd get in touch with me again if they needed me, but confident that their commitment to each other was strong enough for them to find their own way forward and do what was best for their union.

As couples preparing for a commitment to each other sort through some of life's most vexing and troubling questions, it seems those queries boil down to one basic question: "What does it mean to love another person?" It may come as a surprise but in most of the conversations I have with couples before they marry they rarely mention the word, *love*. Love is the force to be reckoned with in moments of major life transitions. Love arrives in the simplest, most powerful forms: standing at the altar or just walking in the park, bidding farewell to a loved one at a grave or receiving a new baby into your arms and recognizing in her perfect face with the characteristic dimple that her grandfather had in the same exact spot on his cheek, a flash of the divine. Love holds even the most challenging aspects of being married.

Young adults are particularly poised to truly fall in love. Do any of us remember the first time we fell for someone? How out of control we felt? How utterly and completely undone we were by the power of infatuation? I have the deep privilege of being in a setting where this is as much a part of the daily life of those I work with as their athletic or academic involvements or their decisions about their life's work. I can be in my office working on a sermon or preparing a report when a student comes through the door breathless, eyes alive, face flushed. I have seen it often enough to know that they are there to share with me that the crush they spoke of a few weeks before had turned into a coffee date and a long walk in the Minnesota night. This palpable joy is something to behold. Its insistent pleasure is nothing but grace—coming often when we least expected it and asking that we open heart, hand, spirit to receive it. A student learns he or she can't earn it. And as in the grace of God, not despite all the warts, moles, neurosis, running leaps at the good, missing the mark, are we loved, but because these very human qualities make us all the more lovely.

I could not have ever predicted how my own intimate love would come to me. I had come through a two-year long journey of healing. In the combined experiences of facing off with the rapist in the police lineup, saying no to what I experienced as the confines of the Baptist denomination of my childhood, and claiming a new denomination by becoming Presbyterian and joining the very church where I was raped, I found new freedom and amazing confidence. The veil lifted as I now named myself as a "rape survivor"—recognizing the significance of this move from "victim" to "survivor," one whose life had been touched by the hand of community, the hand of God, and the loving gaze of Jesus. Heading into my final year at Princeton, I felt alive in ways I hadn't since before the rape. I was ready to finish seminary and seek out a career as a Presbyterian minister.

One afternoon soon after the start of classes, I was eating lunch in the cafeteria with some other of my seminary classmates who had returned from their year-long internships. Our conversation focused on how incredibly different we felt coming back to seminary with a year of full-time ministry under our belts. We looked around at the sea of other students and noted how young, fresh, and naïve they seemed to us. As we gazed around the cafeteria, I noticed another internship returnee, Tom, looking somewhat lost with his tray in his hand. I got up from the table and invited him to join us. The worried look on his face melted away as he set his tray on the table and we all happily reunited with him.

That fall I lived off-campus in Trenton, New Jersey. I had opted to live with other seminary students in a cooperative house in an urban neighborhood. All of us did our field studies in congregations in Trenton and commuted to Princeton for our academic work. I felt quite grown up, ready to tackle the last requirements for graduation. That semester I signed up for a class offered to returning seniors who had spent a year in an internship. Tom was in that class. Up to then, I knew him mainly as the friend of another friend. He was a quiet guy, sensitive and caring, but I didn't know much about him.

That fall I had continued to see Jim Loder for counseling. One afternoon in my session, Dr. Loder and I circled around to talk about the fear

I carried of "men in general." We had spent some hours in therapy dealing with my sense that all men, in my eyes, had the potential to be rapists.

"Lucy, it is probably too much for you at this stage to try to trust men in general," he said one day. "But God's love for you is particular and not general. Maybe you should start with gaining the trust of one or two men."

It seemed like a reasonable suggestion. Taking a more focused approach to trust seemed a safer way of approaching men in general. Loder suggested that I find a friend or acquaintance that I could talk with about what it was like to be a man in the contemporary culture. Though I hesitated, I agreed to do this. I remember leaving his office thinking, "Okay, honestly, what man at Princeton Theological Seminary might be open to discussing what it is like to be a man?" I also had to admit that I didn't really care all that much what men thought about their reality. From my perspective, they had it made. They had ready access to power, positions, jobs in the church, simply because they had the right equipment—that is, the equipment that made them resemble Jesus. But this was my assignment and I was so reliant on Dr. Loder's guidance by that point that openly disregarding one of his suggestions would have felt devastating to me. So dutifully, though doubtfully, I kept myself open to finding a candidate who might be open to my questions about modern American manhood.

I had no luck until late one Friday evening a few weeks later. I had spent the afternoon leaf peeping in rural New Jersey with a group of seminary friends that included Tom. When we got back to campus, the other friends peeled off to their evening engagements. It was about dinnertime and Tom asked if I would like to grab dinner with him. "Sure," I said.

We headed to the cafeteria. As I think back on that evening, there was nothing particularly intimate about the setting—the trays and institutional cooking hardly made for a romantic dining experience—but we had a nice time together. Tom was a great listener, and even in my state of distrust towards his gender, I recognized that he was unquestionably a good guy. He told me about his year doing ministry in a prison in Philadelphia. Tom had supported a very interesting young man named Barry as he transitioned from prison to finding a job. I was impressed with Tom's commitment and care for this young black man who was very gifted and also quite vulnerable.

At some point in the conversation, Tom mentioned that he had been in Dr. Loder's classes. He told me that Dr. Loder had really helped him navigate his relationship with Barry when he was released from prison.

In retrospect, I think it was the knowledge that he respected Dr. Loder as much as I did that allowed me to be more open with him.

In any case, we sat and talked until dinner service ended. As the cafeteria lights started switching off around us, I found myself telling Tom about Dr. Loder's assignment to me. "Yeah, he asked me to talk with a guy about what it is like to be a man," I said. Before I thought about how it might sound to him I added, "And I guess you are someone who might have a perspective on that."

It never occurred to me that I might be asking something from Tom that would make him, as a very introverted Philadelphian, very uncomfortable. I have what I think is a midwestern tendency to venture into most conversations with the assumption that most people are pretty open, to just throw an idea or two out there and figure that even random people will be willing to talk. Maybe it was my lack of pretense or a shortage of developed social cues, but especially in my early years, I often bungled my way into conversations with more reserved or private people, not aware of how I was offending their sense of propriety. In any case, it wasn't until I looked at his face and noticed that the color had faded from it that I suddenly realized that I was asking this guy I barely knew about a region of his experience he may never before have shared with anyone. He grew quieter than he had been—and given that he was already a quiet guy, this meant he was really, *really* quiet. Finally, he spoke. "Okay," he said. "Sure, I am glad to give you some of my thoughts."

The cafeteria worker came to our table and asked for our trays. Taking this as our cue to finally leave, we stood up. Tom suggested we go to his room to continue our conversation. "Great," I said. Despite my having blundered my way into this conversation, now I was nervous too.

As we made our way up the steps to his room, I began to realize that this topic could take us into territory I wasn't sure I was comfortable with. *Was he misconstruing my motives?* I wondered. And then the next jarring thought: *What were my motives? Was I being fully honest with him? Or even with myself?* I pushed the thought out of my mind. *No,* I told myself, *this is all about completing Dr. Loder's assignment.* I focused on the fact that Tom had consented to talk with me about his experience as a man, despite his obvious shock at my having raised the topic. He was also being incredibly respectful, never asking me why I was seeing Loder or probing in any way, a discretion I very much appreciated.

When we arrived at his room, we plopped down on the couch. He had one of the prized two-room suites, an apartment-style arrangement with one room as a study/living room and the other a bedroom. It was a simple space, sparse, slightly shabby but clean. I vaguely recall sharing with him a few things about my work with Dr. Loder. As quickly and lightly as I could, I mentioned the "assault," I think I called it. I explained that in the course of therapy, Loder had suggested that speaking with a man about his experience of being a man would give me some perspective.

"I hope you are okay with talking about this," I said, as a matter of factly as I could.

"Yes, it's fine. Really," Tom said. I heard the tentativeness in his voice, but I believed him. I guessed that this was probably not exactly the way he wanted to spend a Friday evening, but seminary is an odd place—a typical Friday night might include student prayer meetings or a dorm-room rehearsal for a concert of madrigal music, or more often, the every-campus pastime of getting stoned or drunk, undertaken here with a huge measure of associated guilt. In this context, an evening of intense, personal conversation wasn't so far out of the ordinary. Tom was willing to share, and I was a ready listener.

As he looked at me expectantly, I suddenly realized that I had not exactly prepared a set of interview questions. Undaunted, I launched in with no script. I asked a simple question: "What is it like for you to be a man at this seminary?"

He began a bit haltingly, with a couple of generalizations about how awkward he felt when women directed their anger at his gender towards him as an individual. "I must be a safe target for a lot of women's anger because I sure get more than my share of it!" He paused at that and held my eye. But when he saw that I wasn't planning to turn this into a political debate and was still earnestly listening, he went on.

Having had several close friends in college who were African American, he said, he understood to some extent just how challenging it is for those who find themselves at the margins of society or of a community to feel included and to have their contributions fully valued. He went on to share a bit more about his involvement with Barry when he was a prison chaplain.

"You think black people have it tough in this society—try being black and having a prison record! *Really tough.* I realize that as a white guy I don't have those obstacles. People just assume I am going to offer what they expect from a pastor because I am male and white and, I guess, fit their image of a minister."

I was surprised by his honesty and I also was surprised that he had so much to say on the topic. Before this evening, I had known Tom only as the quiet, nice, caring friend of my friend, Jan. As he talked, I tried to remember exactly what Jan had told me about him. I knew little about his background, where he grew up, or his family, but those details felt unimportant in the face of what I was now learning about him.

At some point, I glanced out the window over Tom's shoulder and saw with surprise that it was night. Time was sailing by. When I brought my focus back to him I noticed he was staring at me. Suddenly self-conscious, I did what I had learned to do whenever I felt uneasy: ask another question.

"So, what about you personally, in your own life. What is it like to be a man? Do you find it challenging? "

Again, there was a pause. Then with a new forthrightness he said, "Yes, as a matter of fact I do. I am not very athletic and I grew up in a family that assumed that being athletic is really important, especially for guys, and what is more, that it comes naturally to you. I went to a high school with a bunch of jocks and I wasn't one. It was really hard to be viewed as a klutz. I dreaded those fitness tests." He chuckled, "I would try to fake being sick to avoid going to school on the days when we had them. I would panic when they chose teams for sports. Another really non-athletic guy, Mark, and I were always the last to be picked."

The conversation went on, covering topics from sports to expectations of men to be the initiator in relationships with women, to fear of rejection and so on. I don't know what I had expected, but the conversation offered much more perspective than I had anticipated. I realized that we were *really* talking. After a while, we came to a lull. There was a long moment and then he smiled. "Is this what you are looking for?" he asked.

"I really don't know what I am looking for, but this is really helpful," I said, honestly.

We sat in silence. He was staring at me again but I didn't find it uncomfortable. Finally I looked at my watch and saw with shock how late it had gotten. We had been talking for four hours. I had to get back home to Trenton. I got up to leave, thanking him for the amazing conversation. What happened next, at least from my perspective, was a huge surprise to me—and, I learned later, to him as well. He stood silently for a moment watching me put my coat on. Then I heard him say, "May I kiss you?"

I was taken aback. I remember standing there for a moment, speechless.

"I mean, if you don't mind, I . . . " Tom said.

"Yes," I said in a voice I hardly recognized—thin and almost childlike. He leaned toward me with what struck me more as gratitude than passion, and kissed me very lightly on the lips. When this went over well, he leaned in again for a second, slightly more daring one. I remember looking up into his eyes afterward, aware that a tear was on my cheek. At first I thought it had dropped from my eye, but it occurred to me that maybe it had come from his. I guess I will never know whose tear marked my face that night.

In the days that followed, we were rarely apart. A little over a year later, we were married.

Everyone has their own story about the relationship that changed their lives and how it began, but for me, part of the experience of falling in love with the man who would become my husband was also an experience of discovering another dimension of vocation. In this case, the vocation to love . . . to love God, to love the whole of creation, to love thy neighbor, to be a lover. It happened so simply, and yet, to love is the greatest honor a human being can have. I am completely convinced of this fact. For some, love is a sought-after reward for the hard work of being good, being convincing, or being a certain way for that one certain person. But love's remarkable gift is that giving love, making love, centering love on another, entering love with another person and holding the way open for such a perfect gift requires one thing only—that we receive it. And the odd thing about it is that giving it away is a necessary component of having it fully.

The expansive nature of love not only led me to my own experience with an amazing life partner, but my vocation as chaplain gives me the opportunity to witness moments of love, joy, and beauty that literally take my breath away. Love not only arrives as a gift of grace but it also is something that needs attention. I know this from my own marriage, where there have been plenty of times when the two of us, both very strong people with deeply held convictions, have had rough patches. But I also have seen it in couples I have married or have counseled.

I think of couples like Jamie and Hal, who had hit a snag in planning their ceremony and then called back a few weeks later to meet with me. At the meeting they shared that our conversation had led them to realize that though they knew each other really well, there were values they held that were very different from one another. They told me they spent a lot of time talking about the ceremony and they realized that in one of the classes they had taken at Macalester the professor talked about strength analysis in organizational development: "Professor Jameson said that when an organization begins with affirming strengths rather than deficits, it builds capital for its future." They reported that as they discussed the question of including or excluding spirituality in their ceremony they found that they could look at it as a strength. "If whatever it is will advance the positive aspects of our relationship," (in this case, the spiritual dimensions of the wedding ceremony), "we will embrace it. If, on the other hand, the value is something that distracts or takes away from the relationship such as limiting or stifling the ceremony, we will discard it." I told them that this was a lovely resolution to their dilemma. It made sense for them and I respected not only the outcome but also the process that led them there. I reflected, as I often do, that the couples I work with at the college are so much savvier than I was at that age. When I think about Jamie and Hal's brief moment of conflict in my office and the remarkable way they resolved it, I realize that academic study is not the only mind-blowing aspect of a college education. Learning to treasure, respect, and honor another person is also a remarkable outcome for a college-educated young person.

Indeed, college relationships are good practice for the long-term ones that arrive months or years later. A few years ago, an unexpected email took me across the vast Atlantic Ocean to officiate at a wedding ceremony that held such beauty my heart soared. The email was from a former student who had graduated from Macalester and was now living in her native country of Sweden. Ingrid was a wonderful student and I had enjoyed our long conversations about her life's dreams. Like so many international student alumni, she had graduated, returned to her country of origin, and moved on with her life. Except at the occasional Macalester reunion, I don't hear from many international students unless they need a reference from me. So when the email arrived carrying the question, "Do you do premarital counseling . . . across the globe?" I realized she was announcing her engagement. I hastily read the rest of the note.

"I am engaged to Hans, a wonderful Swedish biologist," she wrote. I could feel her joy coming through the computer screen.

I wrote back with congratulations, saying that, though it might be challenging to have a premarital conversation via Skype or some other means, I'd be open to the idea. We began to consider options.

By amazing coincidence, a few months after Ingrid's query I happened to travel to Sweden and got back in touch with her. We were able to meet up in Stockholm. It was wonderful to see her again and I was very happy to meet Hans. We spent a beautiful evening talking, over herring and other unpronounceable fish dishes, in a wonderful restaurant. Their wedding was planned for a year later. That night, they asked if I would consider officiating. In my wildest dreams I never thought it would work out. But it did.

The following summer, Tom and I flew from St. Paul to Stockholm and made our way to Uppsala. I planned to meet up with Ingrid and Hans on Friday to finalize details for the next day's ceremony. It was a splendid morning. As I sat in the hotel lobby, waiting for them to arrive, I held a third cup of coffee in my hand, jittery from lack of sleep and nervous excitement for what lay ahead. I had officiated at dozens of weddings in my thirty-plus years as a chaplain and each had held its own magnificent beauty but I had never performed a ceremony this far from home or from the familiar. This was different, new, and yet had so much in common, with wedding ceremonies in many times and places.

I find there is always a certain formality to these life occasions—weddings, funerals, blessing and naming ceremonies, baptisms. As I waited for Hans and Ingrid, I reflected that this time was no different. I was not there as a friend, a relative, or a contemporary. They had invited me as their pastor, their chaplain. What did that relationship mean for them and for me? I knew that Hans was not religious. Ingrid was, but in a secular way. From our conversations, I knew that having a church ceremony represented for her the spiritual dimension of love. They understood the reality that being married is more than a contract, something more profound than a business or legal arrangement. Ingrid might not name it as sacred, exactly, but she knew that the promises she and Hans would make were, at their core, steeped in a mystery that holds us even when the fabric of our own making tears.

I was still reflecting on this when the bride and groom came rushing through the lobby door. Ingrid glowed but was also flushed. Hans was flushed and nervous as well. "We hope we aren't late. Oh, Lucy, it is so amazing that you came! Thank you so much!" Ingrid greeted me with a hug. We talked for a while. I reassured them that the wedding ceremony is only one very small moment in the larger work of marriage. They knew it was completely normal to be scared half out of your wits to take a step like getting married, especially when our cultures don't offer a lot of support or images of healthy marriages. Their flushed faces, their wide-eyed hope, their lovingly entwined hands, and their simple readiness said it all.

As I sat in the hotel lobby, I realized that a convergence of my work, my calling, and my context was alive and flourishing at that moment. To officiate at such a celebration of love; to hold the anxiety of this very tender moment; to cross the expanse of seas and cultures in a place I never thought I would visit, let alone officiate at a wedding, was astonishing to me. To receive young people from as near as down the street and as far as Sweden is such a wonderful part of being a college chaplain at a place like Macalester. But then to be invited into the lives of young people and their families back at home after they graduate, to see the world that has shaped them, launched them and then received them back, is even more astonishing. I sat on the leather chair drinking in the moment.

The wedding was the next day. And what a day it was! Hot, by Swedish standards, with crystal clear skies and a hint of autumn in the air. And my, oh my, were there brides and grooms all over that fair city! Brides, grooms, little fairy children in their flower girl and ring bearer outfits. Everywhere, every public garden along the winding river, held brides luminous under trains of gauze alongside sweaty grooms. By the time Ingrid and Hans joined the guests at the church, a short distance into the country from the city of Uppsala, they had been negotiating wedding photo sites with all the other wedding parties, literally lining up to have their day remembered. They both had a bit of camera fatigue and were ready to get on to the main event.

The splendid country church was the one that the famous Swedish botanist Linnaeus attended when he was assigning his elaborate Latin names for flowers and categorizing evolutionary notes on animals at his summer home in the fair fields outside Uppsala. The church was exquisite. Rising out of the fields, it was an ancient rural structure but one that still held life and spirit. Unlike so many churches in Europe whose long histories make them seem, at least to American eyes, more like a play-set than an active house of worship, this was a working congregation.

I was to officiate with a Swedish priest and to my delight it was a woman, a bit younger than myself. She came racing in for the service, explaining that she had had another engagement just prior and would be leaving again directly after the ceremony for yet another one. She had brought a spare chasuble, a white clergy robe, for me. And then to our absolute amazement, we both pulled out the clergy vestment, the long stole we had chosen for the day—I from my closet in Minnesota, her from a wardrobe in her grand office. The stoles were identical. We had a wonderful laugh over that. She was gracious, welcoming and honestly very glad for my coming.

We stepped from the vestibule to the altar area to signal we were ready for the ceremony to begin. A hush fell over the crowd and the organ's last notes faded. The doors of the church opened and the families processed down the aisle, followed by the attendants. Then, with little pomp, the bride and groom, Ingrid and Hans, came up the aisle. There was no huge procession. No music. They simply came to the altar to be married.

There were lots of nerves; sweat dripping from groom, priest, pastor, and even a drip from the bride. But there was a full measure of joy, a few laughs, a deep sense of gratitude for family that was there and for those who weren't—grandparents who were too infirm to come and a grandfather, Henry, who had passed away.

I have officiated at weddings where you feel the space stiffen when there are unresolved issues or family tension or something else in the room that needs to breathe or grab for a lot of elbow room. There are also weddings where you have the keen sense that the church or chapel or garden gives those gathered a wonderful hug, gathering the scattered pieces of history, of other relationships, of hurt and harboring of concern, into communion, where the place itself is holding the scene with deep reverence and deeper joy. This wedding was characterized by the latter. The veil between heaven and earth, the veil that often dims our view, was lifted for a moment.

Veils not only lift to reveal faces full of grace in wedding ceremonies but there are times when a hand lifts the veil to light our way through personal crises. It is the glimmer of some new possibility that arises out of the dark night of the soul. It is a moment when someone believes in you or sees something in you that you don't see yourself that powerfully lifts the eye to new life.

New love was buzzing through the Swedish church as Ingrid and Hans exchanged their vows. They pushed rings onto each other's fingers. They kissed. They held each other a little longer than I usually see, and I found myself giving thanks to God for the privilege of having my eyes feast on such delight, to offer a blessing from their Creator who gave them their life and who so longs for them, for us to love each other, and to know that they are never, ever alone in this journey they began that day. This is the gift we are given as chaplains.

Down the aisle they glided as if they were skating on sheer and glimmering ice. They went out the sanctuary door to the party on the other side. And I wondered at that moment whether the angels that drew close in the sanctuary went with them. I think they were there . . . nothing separates us from the love of God.

I think the vocation of chaplaincy is also about love. It is about loving one's work, loving ideas, loving the way students love their lives. It comes in encounters with couples like Hal and Jamie who are taking their vocation to be married and to love very seriously. And though they may not agree with each other about what spirituality or religion is or isn't, they know it is important to get it right. They, like so many couples, stand together facing the challenges of our times. They discover that this requires strength and resilience. Love harbors both of these. I also find love in my work with those who stand before me professing their love to one another. In the moments when I accompany couples through the thicket of conflict and into the spacious light of honest confession and resolution, I feel so grateful for this work. Or at other times when couples take their classroom knowledge and put it to good use in their relationships, such as Jamie and Hal did, I can only say I am astonished. And at times when I simply am there to witness joy, love and beauty, it is a deep privilege.

I also know that when the veil lifts, when the door shuts in my office, or when the door of the church opens, the doors of the heart also open to summon the strength, courage, and bounty of what takes up residence there. And I offer what I have learned to young adults as they step over the threshold from young adulthood to adulthood. From my own life, I know the surprise of a friend becoming a lover and then life partner. After thirty-plus years of marriage, we still get lost in conversation.

CHAPTER 11

Thresholds of Surprise

Taken to New Places

"Seeing with the eyes of the heart . . ."

Ephesians 1:18

I WAS IN MY office one afternoon a few years ago, when someone knocked very tentatively. I turned to see a student standing there, smiling shyly.

"Are you the chaplain?" she asked.

"Yes," I said, getting up.

"Do you have a minute . . . I mean, is this a good time to talk? If you have office hours, I can come then."

"Oh, no, of course I have time. Please come in."

She came in and sat down, setting her backpack down on the floor and folding her hands in her lap. I took a seat across from her.

"I didn't know who to talk to," she began. "I guess you might think this is sort of weird but I had this thing happen this afternoon in my bio lab. I didn't know who to tell. I was going to my dorm after my lab and I saw the light on in the chapel. I was hoping you'd be here."

I couldn't tell whether she was about to cry or laugh. There was an odd joy around the edges of her mouth. Her eyes glistened as she shyly caught my eye.

"Tell me, what happened?"

"Well, I was working my lab, like I've done every week for this class. I was looking through the microscope at this cell. And then . . ." She paused and looked up at me, eyes shining. "Oh, chaplain, I was suddenly struck by the marvel of it. . . . It was just so amazing, so magnificent, so beautiful. As I stood there looking at it, I just started to giggle. My lab partner looked at me like I was crazy and I felt kind of stupid. But I couldn't get the thought out of my mind. *God made that cell*, I kept thinking, and it was absolutely gorgeous. I mean, it just seemed so amazing."

"Wow," I said, genuinely delighted by her story but also by the fact that she'd decided to share it with me. "That is really amazing!"

We both sat silently for a moment. I honestly didn't quite know what else to say. I suddenly realized that I hadn't even asked her name. She hadn't offered it.

"I'm so sorry, but I didn't ask your name, nor did I introduce myself. I'm Lucy."

"Oh, I know who you are," she said. "I remember your prayer at that new student convocation we had. My name is Jenny."

I smiled at her. "Jenny, yes, this is an amazing moment. I am so grateful to you for coming here to tell me about it."

"Oh, I am so relieved," she said. "I thought of telling my professor about it, but I didn't think he'd understand. I thought if I told my lab partner, she'd think I was nuts."

"Why did you think your professor might not understand?" I asked.

"Well actually, it seems like no one here is religious. I mean, you might know a few religious people, but professors never talk about things like religion, or God. I am not a creationist or anything like that, though kids in my high school were. But when I was looking through that microscope, something clicked. It was like seeing the whole universe in that little cell." She sat quietly for a moment, the look of wonder still shining on her face.

"That is really a powerful insight," I said. "What did you see?"

"I don't know, just . . ." She collected her thoughts. "To think that out of that very small, immensely small, unit, all of life is constructed. It is so fragile and yet so terse. It is infused with messages; it speaks, sort of . . . I can't fully describe it," she said. "But as I looked at it more, I just felt such joy. I guess that was the giggle." She smiled—mostly to herself, but in a way that made me feel lucky to be included.

Part of my delight in this welcome interruption to my afternoon was my amazement that Jenny was so articulate about what she had experienced.

She was able to describe lucidly an experience that other people throughout the centuries have found themselves silenced by. I saw her astonishment. And in it, I also recognized my own experience of encountering great mystery at a very tender age.

I began to speak and she looked up. "Do you know the word *mystic* as it's used in the religious sense?" I asked her. "Usually it refers to people who see God's presence in the world in surprising, immediate ways. I think I might call your experience a mystical experience."

Jenny's face went flush. I thought she might be worried about something I'd said. "Does that concern you?" I asked.

"Oh, no," she said. "My grandfather would often talk about how he was a water witch. He could go around with one of those sticks and find water. People thought he was odd but he definitely wasn't crazy or making it up. I wonder if I got some of his genes. You know, like being open to things that don't make sense but yet you know them." She paused, considering this.

"Yes! I would say that is worth exploring," I said.

We sat quietly for a moment, catching our breath, allowing the rush of all that had transpired settle over us.

A thought occurred to me. "Jenny, would you consider talking with your professor about what happened?" I asked. At her hesitation, I asked her who the professor in the lab was. When she told me, I didn't know the name—it was someone who was filling in for a professor on sabbatical.

"Do you think he'd understand?" she asked.

"Well honestly, I don't know Professor Wagner, but I'd actually encourage you to talk with him about it, Jenny. I know several of the professors in biology and I actually think this kind of experience may happen more often than you think," I said.

"Really? Do you think so? I don't know. It just seems like something a chaplain would get more than a professor," she said.

I laughed. "Well, I get the God part but I did pretty poorly in my cell biology class in college. Your professor has probably dedicated his life to examining the beautiful cell you were so amazed by."

"I might bring it up . . . I don't know. But actually, I think I will start with my lab partner. She is funny and she might sort of get it," Jenny said.

"That seems like a good start."

She started to collect her things. "I really need to go, but thanks." She paused before walking out the door. "As I said before, I'm really glad you were here."

I thought about our conversation for the rest of the afternoon. Jenny had witnessed mystery in the divine sense, almost like what the mystics describe when they see the universe in an acorn or the glory of God in the universe. She had this experience in a college lab, of all places. It haunted her enough for her to slip by my office to tell me about it. I had watched as she made her way down the hallway toward the chapel door, almost dancing. To another observer, it might have looked eccentric, but I thought a dance, a jig, a high-step was the right response to the spiritual wonder she'd just experienced.

Jenny was not the first person to arrive at my door eager to share a powerful insight. If I had been the lucky audience to more than a few of these moments of awe, how many more must be happening on a campus at any given moment? The enterprise of higher education is designed to encourage "aha" revelations, openings through which an insight or idea or truth about life can rise up from underfoot, padding its way into consciousness. Its appearance often surprises the witness, particularly when the insight takes one to the territory of great truth.

Because I've seen the power that these sudden, unexpected insights have in the lives of those who have experienced them, I've begun to think about how they fit into my professional context. As chaplain, it's part of my role to care for the spiritual lives on my campus; maybe more importantly, I hold one of the institution's only roles overtly assigned to the important work of acknowledging mystery, as Jenny so clearly demonstrated by knocking on my door, guessing correctly that she and her message would be welcomed. How can I best support and encourage these moments of mystery, insight, and connection that are so vital to healthy intellectual life?

One of the metaphors that has been most helpful to my thinking over the years comes from the world of theater. A few years after I began working there, Macalester hosted a performance and workshop by an acquaintance of mine, the dancer Judith Rock, whose Body and Soul Dance Company was well known in the Bay Area's theology and arts movement.

The night she and her dance partner, Phil, arrived on campus it was in the middle of a bitter cold, full-blown Minnesota winter. After the hugs and small talk about their travels, they changed into their lycra, moved chairs out of the carpeted room and rehearsed with me their plan for the workshop. They were singularly focused, serious dancers, who excitedly awaited the arrival of the student participants. After a few minutes the students, mostly women but a few men, ventured in and the workshop began.

I don't remember much about the workshop but I remember being enthralled by Phil's description of the guerrilla theatre movement of the 1960s and its influence on their work. He described events in which an actor would, without warning, suddenly break into a soliloquy or public conversation or mime in a public place. At first the bystanders, whether in a restaurant, a park, a shop, or the university cafeteria, would assume it was a naturally occurring moment—an argument or just people being crazy. When they started to realize that something more was underway, confusion would reign for a moment. But then, once it became evident that the event was quite planned, the "audience" suddenly became anyone who was willing to give him or herself over to the interruption. Those who opted to stay and pay attention found themselves pulled out of an ordinary day into a moment of wonder, becoming participants in a work of art they would never have imagined just minutes earlier.

As Judith and Phil talked more, I couldn't get an idea out of my head: Might chaplaincy function something like this guerrilla theater? I wouldn't meet Jenny for a few more years, but I had already seen times and places on campus when, arising out of the commonplace, a student or faculty member saw something that jarred the imagination. What if, in the daily life of a college, the chaplain could nudge these experiences into being, maybe by just directing students' attention to the moments happening at the margins of experience, out of the corner of the eye—never exactly straight ahead, but noticed from an angle, at the edges of something else. In these otherwise overlooked eruptions of grace, might they see something more profound? A meeting of mind and heart? The universe? God?

"Guerrilla chaplaincy." It seemed a preposterous possibility, one just bizarre enough to be relevant. What I meant by the term had less to do with the "guerrilla tactics" the theater movement borrowed its concept from, but was more a way of describing and encouraging the way that faith dawns: that it seems to come with a slant of light, with the calling from stars, from the beauty of a loving moment, from the realization that life as we know could be swept away, from the entry of the unexpected into the world of the unsuspecting. And though when someone encounters disruption or surprise, the human instinct is to batten down the hatches and shore up the framework to keep the invading or inviting Presence at bay, I kept thinking of all the people who, once they realized they were in the midst of a theatrical performance, *didn't* hurry along but paused to let themselves be absorbed and changed by it. I wanted to help foster a campus environment where moments of wonder and awe would not just be present but welcomed.

In his book of prayers, *Guerrillas of Grace,* writer and minister Ted Loder (coincidentally, a cousin of my seminary mentor, Dr. Jim Loder) provides a rich and imaginative angle on this idea. Loder notes, "Somewhere I read a description of poets as 'guerrillas of beauty' . . . I began to see 'guerrillas of beauty' as applying to the risky and exciting struggles of people attempting to live out their faith in more free and joyful ways in the midst of difficult, resistant, often even oppressive circumstances."[1] Sometimes young adults like Jenny find the faith they carry into the college context shaken or challenged by the silence of faith in the academy. Though they might not name their experience in such dramatic terms viewed as resistant or even oppressive, they do hesitate to claim the power of insight, of reaching minds that stumble onto mystery. What would it be like if campuses not only accepted the grand insight into mystery but found ways to heighten the power of such remarkable and joyful moments, recognizing them as givens in every sense of that word?

Ministry on a secular campus is a guerrilla enterprise as it often catches even those more "ready" for spiritual life off guard. When something doesn't really compute, such as seeking the mystery of life in a cell or sensing a connection to a loving God at a time when I was so angry about the rape, it requires that we acknowledge the experiences and allow ourselves to be changed by them. Though you honestly never know where a grand and transformational insight will show up, when the yearning for deep life will awaken, or who might be knocking at your door, a person like Jenny reminds you that the holy can make itself known in the least expected moments. Often I am as surprised as anyone when it does.

Part of what is so important for students is the art of accepting such abandon and the attending surprise that may arrive. I have witnessed such moments in others. I have been swept up in them myself.

For me, my call to become a minister—and the way and place I came to be ordained—could not have surprised me more. Over my last year of seminary I entered the process of ordination in the Presbyterian Church. Hebrew language was required for ordination, as was Greek. I had already taken Greek, so I arranged to take Hebrew from a rabbi in Zanesville, Ohio, a small town near to my first position at Muskingum College.

1. Loder, *Guerrillas of Grace,* 7.

Though I was living in Ohio, the tradition was that the ordination service would take place at the church where I was a member. I flew to Seattle to meet with the committee for ordination candidates. I took ordination examinations. I wrote endless drafts of my statement of faith. And finally, after I had met all the requirements, I was examined by a hundred-plus ministers and lay elders. They grilled me on the "floor of Presbytery" (not literally down on the floor but there were moments when I felt like they were pinning me down), asking theologically nuanced questions as well as questions about how I would apply my knowledge to practical situations.

I was, after all, the first woman to be ordained by this particular region of Presbyterians. After an unprecedented forty-five-minute examination, an elderly minister stood up in the back of the church. When he was called on to speak, he said in a kind but firm way, "Young lady, if I had been subjected to the kind of questioning you have been given today, I would not be a Presbyterian minister. I move that the questioning be arrested!" I smiled at him and whispered, "Thank you."

I left the room and in short order was escorted back in with loud applause. I was slated to be ordained the very next day.

I will never forget the ordination service. It was Super Bowl Sunday, 1980. The Philadelphia Eagles were playing the Oakland Raiders, but the game was the last thing on my mind. Through the years since the rape I had journeyed through anger at God, rage at men and the institutions that sustained their power and privilege. I had found remarkable friends and mentors who not only supported my emotional and spiritual healing but also encouraged me to take the bold step of hearing God's call to be ordained. I carried in my soul the burden of knowing that there were likely other young women and men who had experienced trauma and found themselves alone to deal with them. And I also knew that I had been blessed by the love and care of mentors and the powerful healing of God, who had accompanied me through the "toil and snares" of the past years and had loved me, held me and, with a surprising grace, called me to be a minister.

Jack and Barbara's church, now mine too, had utterly transformed for me over the past years. It had become a congregation that I got to know by joining it and that, in turn, got to know me. We had come to love one another. This beloved congregation was thrilled to host the service. And as it turned out, it was a day filled with joy and symbolism, as it would be for any young minister. But for me, the ceremony would carry a particular poignancy.

In the weeks and months after the rape, would I have ever dreamed that I would join the very church where it occurred? Would I have even fleetingly considered being ordained in the church sanctuary not fifty steps from the place where I thought I would die? Though I had made the decisions that had brought me here, I couldn't help but feel humbled by God's hand in this extraordinary turn of events.

Of course, most of the congregation assembled that day didn't know the terrible story that had brought me closer to the Wilsons and, eventually, their church. They did know, however, that I was to be the first woman ever ordained in that cluster of thirty or so Presbyterian churches in the Northwest region of Washington State. Because that made it a historic event for the larger community too, those planning the service of ordination decided to couple it with a seminar on feminist theology. That afternoon thirty or forty congregants came to hear a panel of women ordained in other Christian churches talk about developments in inclusive language, women in leadership, new interpretations of biblical scholarship, and Jesus' advocacy for women in the Gospels.

Following the seminar, about a hundred people gathered in the modern sanctuary of Maplewood Presbyterian Church. I was the only person being ordained that day. My parents had come from Iowa, my friends living in the area were all there, plus the church officials had gathered, robed in their Sunday best, ready to surround me with the hands of ordination.

Words of greeting began the service. We sang my favorite hymn. Jack Wilson, my pastor and friend, gave a sermon on the importance of being a pioneer for the faith. His thoughts were eloquent, generous, compelling. My new spouse, Tom, who was himself a freshly minted Presbyterian pastor, delivered a charge to me that included some stories about my childhood. He embarrassed me a bit with one about how, as a seven-year-old, I accompanied my parents to their church bowling league at a local alley. While they were bowling, I would, unbeknownst to them, go up to people who were enjoying a beer and smoking cigarettes, and tell them that God didn't want them to drink beer or smoke. A child evangelist was what Tom called me. I chuckled along with everyone, realizing that the seeds of conviction had long been planted in my young frame and that they were still alive on this afternoon so many years later.

My friends Jan and Julie spoke words to me with high and holy reminders that the work I was stepping into is filled with uncertainty, challenge, and a high measure of grace. They also knew my story about the rape and their words about the power of women to say "yes" to what gives life and a powerful "no" to anything that diminishes us roused the congregation to shout out a very energetic, "Amen." They infused their comments with quotes from feminist theologians Mary Daly and Rosemary Reuther. They also lifted my soul with words from Frederick Buechner that had stirred my soul many times before: that "the coronation of Jesus in the believing heart should take place among confession and tears . . . and great laughter."[2] And in that moment I knew I had confessed to a lot of fear and had shed ample tears, but I had no idea that great laughter, bountiful joy, was in the offing.

The moderator of the Presbytery, a woman elder from a congregation down the road, asked me the questions of ordination. The one that sent chills down my spine was, "Will you serve the people with energy, intelligence, imagination, and love?" And my voice trembled when I said, "I will."

But it was the moment when I knelt on the carpeted floor of the sanctuary that I will never forget. The many ministers' and elders' hands on my head and my shoulders seemed to be blanketing me, weighting down my body, but also holding my heart and spirit. With the proclamation that I was now a minister of the gospel of Jesus, I felt the evil of a sick and violent man lose its wrestling match with the power of God's Spirit. I suddenly felt the demon, which had haunted me in that church and in my heart, leave for good. As soon as the hands of ordination lifted from my body, I was filled with such a joyful lightness that for a moment I thought I might actually float out of the church. The long journey from rape to ordination had come through the remarkable call from God through the voice of this community. I dared to answer it. And, in the very moment and place of doing so, I was now free: free to serve, free to grow, free to speak truth, free to be an agent of healing for others.

Who would have thought, dreamed, imagined such a surprise?

It's because I've seen the power of remaining open to surprise even through times when I might have turned away from it out of self-preservation, that I know how transformative it can be in the lives of others.

I have watched it happen with students who have experienced great loss. It takes all their strength to open my office door, their tears spilling, their eyes searching my face or downcast, the stunned silence broken only by low sobs. Often they are far from home. They may be thinking of a parent who is living with compromised health because treatment options are

2. Buechner, *Alphabet of Grace*, 44.

limited. And their questions are "How will I live, now that the very ground of my being has a serious fissure in it?" I am there to listen, to care, and also to help them know they are not alone in their hurt. And I trust that they can feel not only a pastor's love for them, but that they sense that the greatest gift I can give them is my presence and the strength that I have received through God's healing grace.

I have also seen it happen when students receive affirmation beyond their wildest dreams. Bursting through my door with the rush of fevered excitement tipping their faces toward the stars, they can hardly wait to share the news: "I got the job . . . or the A . . . or the internship . . . or forgiven . . ." I rejoice with those who rejoice and weep with those who weep. And though there are the tough times, there are many more of the joy-filled ones. There are times when light filters through the cracks in fear or uncertainty, and it also makes space for the wholeness of life, for our ability to become receivers of the bounty of goodness, to arrive. This is the work of a chaplain, to be there when things get tough, when what seems so certain splits open or when joy bursts out from a seeming hopeless situation.

There are certainly experiences that could drive us to become cynics, casting aspersions on the whole damn mess. But I have to believe that a campus chaplain attending to the fear, the loneliness, the uncertainty that abounds on campus, who won't rule out that even the most stricken human heart, even the most seething spirit, even the disrespectful, despicable act, can be changed. I know that forgiveness can be asked for and given, that the chaplain is living out the guerrilla faith that points the community to and receives the gift of life from the very giver of life. Indeed, right in the midst of these shocking, sorry, pernicious moments on campus, stunning, gracious, sweeping love can arrive in its wake. The Too-Much-For-Words Holy One arises from the mundane life we live, startling even the most ready person with unbridled goodness and holding the tears, fears, and hope itself as a gift to be carried from that gathering into the hard work of facing each other the next day, and the next, and the next.

I hope I am able to hold my heart open in all its surprising goodness, to emerging ideas and ideals of new generations of students, who are on a quest for fullness of life. I deeply desire that I might be a guerrilla chaplain who sets herself squarely in the midst of the established power of institutions and offers a word of grace, underfoot, erupting when least expected, awakening the heart while the mind minds the academic "shop."

Sometimes I feel like the best thing I can do as a chaplain to encourage moments of insight and wonder on my campus, that the best kind of "guerrilla chaplaincy" I can muster, is just to expect holy surprise in my own life and to encourage the same expectation in others. Leave the door ajar, I sometimes advise my students. I need to listen to this as well.

Some months after our first meeting, Jenny arrived at my door for the second time. Her face wore a beautiful smile and she had a little potted crocus in her hand.

"This is for you, chaplain."

"Oh, Jenny, this is so beautiful, thank you!"

"It reminded me of our conversation about the cell. Do you remember?" she asked, almost shyly.

"I do remember," I told her.

"Well, looking at the color of this flower," she gently touched the edge of the crocus, "I thought of beauty and I also realized I didn't tell you about my professor."

"Oh? Did you ever talk with him?" I asked.

"Yes, I did. I told him that I had seen something more than just the cell but something that was holy." Almost as if she couldn't believe it herself she said, "Yeah, I used that word. And he said to me that he'd actually had a similar experience to mine. And it was why he did his graduate work and why he teaches today."

I caught in Jenny's eye the look of someone who would take her love for that cell and her love for the Creator of all cells into every classroom she would go on to teach in. It would be with her in every conversation she would engage in, every hour or week or year that the beauty of life awakened before her. She might never again mention her moment in the lab publicly, but there would be other students, hers and mine, who would find their way to her door and whisper to her their deep reverence of such moments. And they would be stirred by her passion and deep love of her work, by her vocation—not just to practice science, but also to notice, to receive and to giggle with pure joy.

CHAPTER 12

Thresholds of Promise

Faring Well

IT IS A GLISTENING May afternoon in Minnesota. The snow that only a few weeks ago clung to the branches, carried all-wheel-drive vehicles into ditches, and caused a broken hip or two, is now gone. It is commencement day at Macalester College.

That morning, I preached the baccalaureate sermon. It was the fifteenth year I had done so at this College. Each time I have offered a word of send-off to a class through my baccalaureate address, I have been moved by the particular threshold that event takes all of us toward. Even as I draw out the manuscript I've so carefully crafted, I find myself beside myself, really, because words cannot hold the sadness, the anticipation, the keen look over the shoulder, the clear vista ahead for all who sit before me. It is akin to arriving home from a wonderful beach vacation and stepping through the door. The taste of the sea salt is still on the lips, sand crunching in the sneakers, cheeks and shoulders still pleasantly sun-warmed. Going through the door, papers are stacked up on the table, the mail is in a heap, the dog needs attention. But home also represents comfort, familiarity, the daily patterns that accumulate to make a life. At this baccalaureate moment too, coming to the open door of the future with students is like beachcombing—that is, combing the past for joyful recollections while also looking ahead to uncertainty and to finding the comforts of a home place, whether with friends or in a job that asks the very best of you, or a volunteer position that grabs your deepest imagination and joy.

As I stood to give my sermon, I caught the eye of my daughter, Mara, sitting to my left in the choir she had sung in throughout her four years as a Macalester student. It was her graduation day. Along with Mara, her brother and sister, Tom, two grandmothers, her aunt and two uncles were there as well. The text I had chosen to focus my remarks on came from the biblical story of Ruth. (This is the same text I thought of the night with the women in the Threads spirituality circle.) But today I remind those who gathered in the chapel of the three women standing on a plain in a far-off land. Three women whose lives have come unstuck; three women at a crossroads between past and future, between uncertainty and the clear direction dictated by social norms. Three women who make distinct choices: Ruth chooses to stay with her mother-in-law, Naomi. Orpah, the other daughter-in-law, leaves the two and goes off to her family of origin; these were three women who were transitioning from the known of loss to the unknown of possibility.

As I looked into the eyes of my daughter and out towards all of the families gathered, I held the pride of all they had accomplished. I also realized that I was uneasy, wondering whether the world that had seen crashing financial systems in 2008 would be able to offer this graduating class opportunities worthy of their remarkable abilities. I also found myself wondering if the morsel of wisdom I would share with them about what sustains life could withstand the pressing issues that they would encounter as they crossed the threshold from college to the world beyond. But mostly, I was overcome with gratitude that I could stand at this crossroads with young adults.

Besides speaking of the courage of Ruth and Naomi, who stood at a crossroads, I challenged the class of 2009 to cross the threshold of life with awe for the magnificent gifts of the created order and also to cultivate a healthy rebellion, that maverick spirit that is so resident at Macalester College. What I didn't say aloud that day but I knew with every fiber of my being as I stood in that chapel in the presence of my family—both my blood relatives and my campus family—was that I was standing at a threshold that day as well. I was launching my child into the world from Macalester's portal, ending an amazing four years of having her begin her young adulthood in the setting where I work. I was also worried that my future in that place might now hold a certain emptiness without her there.

As I preached the sermon and then exited the chapel, the chill of the day met my unsettled spirit. But there was no denying the celebratory air all around—the buzzing excitement of the streams of students and their families leaving the chapel brushed away the uneasy feelings.

From the chapel sidewalk, I look out onto the campus landscape as I have so many times over the past years on commencement day. The efforts of the grounds crew show in the gussied-up campus: manicured lawn, flowers newly planted around the flagpole, 3,000 chairs arranged in perfect rows, some already claimed by families who want a good view. The nearly 500 diplomas stacked on folding tables await the graduates' ready hands. I meet my family for a quick lunch and then return to the chapel to get ready for the commencement ceremony. I now have my academic gown on, my commencement invocation in hand as the bagpipes ready us all for the ceremony. Somewhere behind me, my daughter is lining up with her classmates, her cap and gown carefully arranged.

When the bagpipe procession is over and everyone is settled in their seats, I offer an invocation to start the ceremony. Then a famous speaker intones famous words with conviction: "Don't let anyone tell you that you can't save the world . . . you must!"

At last it's time for "conferring degrees," aka, giving the students their diplomas. "Class of 2009, please stand," the president says. Shrieks of delight erupt as the first and then the fiftieth and then the four hundred and eighty-fourth graduate crosses a short platform. They are in high form, this class. They are ready to take a giant step toward the new world.

Sometimes faculty parents or trustee parents or grandparents hand their special graduate his or her diploma. My daughter doesn't want me to do this. She doesn't want to be any different than the rest of the class and I respect her decision. But I do stand at the end of the stage, having been there to give the invocation, and fling my arms around her as she makes her way across with her diploma in hand. Such joy!

Finally, the president's says the well-faring words, "Congratulations!" It is over. The roll call is over. The diplomas are distributed, mortarboards flung to high heaven. Beaming faces freeze for photo after photo—taken and then sent via text message to a grandmother in Uganda, a brother in Iraq, an aunt in Vietnam, who couldn't make it to the ceremony. In an instant the celebration has flashed across the globe.

As I leave the stage and process behind trustees and the president down the grassy aisle through the class of 2009, with the cavalcade of bagpipes and drums recessing ahead, I am snagged by just how time caves in on itself. It seems like only a few weeks have passed since taxis left these students at the curb with bags in hand as well as their hopes, dreams, sorrows, regrets, and possibility. Was it really that long ago that I watched the student athlete with her bags unloaded by a brother or boyfriend meet her soccer teammate, pick up her keys and walk down the hallway toward her room, her life? Four years seem to have run underfoot like small children, begging for a lap or a treat or a lingering smile. I hold this afternoon like snapshots, precious in my hand, close to my heart, pausing to wait for the story, the sound, the fury, the hope that reaches from each of them. Snapshots, glimpses, glimmers, small and gargantuan moments; not cinema that rolls over and over with foreground, backdrop, a well-chosen soundtrack, lights . . . action. No, to me there are snapshots. And maybe snapshots are how it should be in this work.

I hold many snapshots in my mind's eye as I think about the multiple callings that I have heard and responded to in my life. I hold that night with the stars erupting before my four-year-old eyes; I see the angular finger of my chaplain as he pointed to the speakers in the campus coffee shop and asked me about Bob Dylan's song; I flash on that bright May day at Macalester when I first interviewed and how that student leaned toward me with her eyes brimming with her vision of my work as a chaplain, her chaplain. I see the face of a parent whose son died on a college-sponsored trip; I see the grins of a new college student's five-year-old twin sisters, looking up into his face and holding extra tight to his hand. But the snapshots accumulate to tell the story of a lifetime call, a storyboard of sorts that add up to my vocational life. My hope lies in the possibility of all of those 484 that crossed the stage that day and in the thousands of others who have crossed or will cross it to become amazing citizens of this, our globe.

Wandering amid the clusters of happy graduates posing with friends and loved ones, I scan the crowd for my own beloved graduate. Stumbling over robes and finally discarded stiletto shoes, I harvest another snapshot out of the bounty of that day.

Could it really have been four years ago? It seems like only a few short months earlier that I stood at another threshold, this time the doorway of Mara's bedroom at home, saying to her, "It's time to start packing." She was off to college in a few short days. This was the child who struggled with transitions, who hung on to the door of the car literally risking her life, when she was left at a day care as a child. She had chosen to go to

Macalester, where I worked. And we had made a contract of sorts, that she would determine her limits and engagements with me. We were both on a journey for which we had no clear directions. I completely respected her needs. I had my place at the College and she was just beginning. When she asked me to get out of the way, I acquiesced. When she needed her mom, I was there. Our connection would deepen over those years, but we didn't know that yet.

That day, I stood in the doorway of Mara's room for the simple reason that the room held so much I couldn't navigate my way in or out. She was opening drawers that contained too-small shirts that had been wadded in the corner for long years; discovering a small handmade clay whistle shaped in the form of a bird, a treasure from her own very small but steady third-grade hand. In tilting piles lay the scores of notebooks full of information that had once seemed absolutely important: the Battle of Gettysburg, iambic pentameter, the first success with long division. All there, silted up like sedimentary layers she was now excavating.

At last the bags were packed and we carried them down the steps and into the car, the large maroon duffle jammed with this and that, all to set sail across the few blocks to her new home at college. That afternoon, I knew that this was only the first of many times I would feel the sand shift under me as her parent. I thought of all these bags, packed now and to be unpacked again in a few hours, the duffels and suitcases remaining just slightly in sight to remind her that college is temporary. Before long, they'd be packed again: for her study abroad in Ghana, then the summer working at a retreat center, and eventually, four short years away, at graduation.

As I search through the crowds of glowing young graduates and their loved ones, a familiar feeling comes over me again, the feeling that I have arrived at a blessed calling and encountered a locked door. A calling can take one to a vista, I have learned, a place of perspective, but it also can take one to the uncertainty and frustration of a lock. But like that cold day when the key was in someone else's hand, so also, I find myself feeling with gratitude that the key to the future—mine, the planet's, God's future—is in the hand of the young people who crossed the stage, attended by chaplains and faculty members, filled with grand insights and ready contributions.

It is an odd thought, more fitting for my daughter and her classmates than for me. But that afternoon I think I hear, amid the buzz of graduates' excitement, those same words: "Go from your country and, your kindred

and your father's house, to a land I will show you." And I think I understand: that land is less of a physical locale, a job change, or a new campus or
a community in which to contribute, and more about letting be, of faring
well, of giving over to the One who promised that old man on that plain
years ago, that the land would be one of none other than milk and honey
and the recipients would outnumber the galaxies.

That word that arrives for me is the same word that haunted my early
call to be chaplain at Macalester College: "Go," says the Lord to Abram.
Yes, that is the word: *Go.* As I work my way through the hugging, smiling,
joy-filled air, I know that I, like Abram, am being called to pull up the stakes
and pitch a tent in a new land.

My vocation as a chaplain is set in a place, a College, where I wait on
the Spirit's light to shine out from the hearts of young adults; where I make
my way each day down a sidewalk, onto campus, down steps with key in
hand, to open that door to everything that comes my way. But my vocation
as a college chaplain is also to propose an alternative narrative to the success narrative that is inherent in higher education.

In order to pay the bills, colleges must promise a good "product" for
the "investment," which is quite steep. That promise manifests itself in a
success narrative: after four years in our institution you will leave to change
the world; you will be one of the elite who will be able to apply to excellent
graduate and professional programs; you will have in hand the tools for the
good life. Rarely does a college talk about the reality that there will be times
of great failure; days when you wonder if you will be able to get out of bed;
times when, through nothing you did, someone crosses a threshold to do
harm to you. The word that I hope I am able to speak through the story of
my life and the practice of care I bring to campus is an alternative narrative to the success narrative. And that alternative story is one that actually
begins with surprise, with grace, with the unexpected and unasked-for experience of deep love from God, the appearance of God on a porch. And it
also has within it episodes when all could have been lost but instead I found
moments when I came to life in ways I could never have expected.

As I wander through the campus searching for my daughter, a group
of graduates, all women who were in a volunteer program I had overseen,
call me over. They introduce me to their parents, who remind me of some
of my friends. Just as the thought crosses my mind, one of the students

quips, "Mom and Dad, this is our chaplain, Lucy. She is the one I said would be your friend if you lived here." Everyone laughs. These are quality human beings who had sent their precious children to us for their education.

With the rush of finals and the week of activities leading up to graduation, I haven't heard what is next for the students. Three of the four are staying in Minnesota for the first year out. Almost as a formality, I tell them that we should find a time to connect. I don't expect to actually follow through, since I rarely see many of the graduates after they leave campus. But I do see these women again.

Six months after we stood on that lawn, I received an email invitation to join up with them for breakfast at a local restaurant. It was a late winter Saturday morning. I remember trying to figure out if I would wear work clothes—a pair of wool slacks and a sweater—or my typical Saturday jeans. I decided, jeans.

I felt uncharacteristically anxious as I entered the restaurant with the three women already halfway through their first cup of coffee. I wasn't quite sure what my role would be with them given that they were no longer students. They weren't friends and they weren't parishioners. They were alumnae of the College and they still thought of me as their chaplain. My discomfort was heightened when, oddly enough, they had traded in their college uniform of jeans for dress-slacks, sweaters, bright scarves in casual loops, and dangly earrings. The sallow complexions of finals week were gone and their bearing was bright, easy, adult. We shared hugs, they ordered me a cup of coffee, and a burst of conversation erupted. They quickly informed me that another friend in New Jersey would be phoning in shortly. "No Skype," one explained, "because it is Saturday and she didn't want to get dressed for the visual effects."

I simply smiled.

A few minutes later the call came from Jill. With the cell phone on speaker mode and the four us of leaning in, communion erupted. We broke bread, poured coffee, our minds relaxing and our hearts beginning to reach for abundant life. I had the deep sense that morning that where two or three are gathered, Christ is indeed there.

The conversation with Jill and the other three was lovely. They spoke together about their longing to be involved with each other's lives. "Who are you seeing? How is the new job? Did you find an apartment? Craigslist, yup, used it often." But there was also a tinge of fear about the future. "If I don't go to grad school next year and work instead, am I closing off possibilities for advancement?" "If Jeff, my partner, gets into med school, should I move with him, stay here?" It is rough being a young adult these days.

At that point Jill had to hang up. Yoga class was calling. When the cell phone was off, there was a pause and their eyes met mine. I knew from many years of conversation with these three that they were waiting for me to guide the conversation. And that morning, as on so many others, I was surprised by their deference. I sipped the burning coffee and asked a question that has been quite present in my own life since coming to Minnesota.

"So, how's it going, finding community here in the Twin Cities? Do you mostly hang out with each other?"

Without hesitation, Jacquie, boldly, clearly, honestly said, "We mostly complain to each other about how hard it is to find new friends. It's so easy when you're in college to meet up with friends. They're down the hall, or across the table in the dining hall, or doing community service with you."

"Yeah," says Maggie, "Now you have to work at finding connections."

The quietest of the three at the table, Kira, said, "It's easy to give up on finding friends or making contacts—business and personal. So, Lucy, I did something really radical. You may be surprised, but I actually went to church." I smiled, mostly because I wasn't surprised at Kira. Like all of these women, she knows the power of community, whether in church or yoga or dance or intellectual circles. But as they talked that day, I realized that of all the things we teach at college, in the end, all the of hours cultivating critical thinking skills, deconstructing airtight arguments, the day-in, day-out probing of universals, all give way to the very simple act of walking into a room of strangers and learning how to simply say, "Hello, I'm Kira. Who are you?"

Kira spoke of going to Trinity Lutheran Church, a small congregation, and after many weeks finally finding a small foothold in the choir. Focusing on her contributions, being engaged by the sense of Christian care and also simply wanting to be there, over time she noted that community has a way of sneaking up, tapping a shoulder from behind, only to plant the kiss of peace on a cheek.

Jacquie and Maggie were roommates and stayed more in touch with friends in the Twin Cites. Jacquie was a freelance artist and Maggie a dancer. They told me that they were starting a dinner club using the slow food movement as their theme. They had both gotten a community garden plot and were excited to grow fruits and vegetables. "We'll have you and Tom over some night, Lucy."

"I'll drop everything to come!" I said.

That graduation day on the Macalester College lawn, I snapped a photo of the four of them with their parents. Their parents traded places with me and I was then in the photo with the four. I had accompanied these students and many more on the lawn that day through some of the most emotionally rocking situations they had faced in their short lives: break-ups, the death of a friend, family turmoil, uncertainty about whether they should go into teaching or ministry or neither. I stood smiling into a camera, but I also wrapped my arms around them, not knowing what would come of them, or what would come of me. This thing called an alma mater, which literally means "bounteous mother," binds our lives. The bounty comes to me often, but this particular day, it comes with extravagance and haunting grace.

"Have you bumped into Mara?" I asked the three.

"Yes, we saw her with her friends, Paul and Aurora," they replied. "I think they are by the Campus Center." I continued to wander the grounds looking for Mara and my family members. I began to grow frustrated by not finding them. I was mad at myself for not setting a specific place we might meet, to collect ourselves. I always thought of this campus as a small place but today, with 3,000 people making their way from the ceremony to the refreshments, it seemed like a vast place.

I headed the way the students pointed and in a moment, a very short moment, I spotted the ones on whom I hang the sun, moon and stars—the faces of my spouse, my children, and their grandmothers, there beaming with joy and promise, of milk and a lot of honey! They were lining up for photos. My heart leapt with joy to see them. I hugged Mara; the grandmothers hugged me. The joy of the multiple vocations I inhabit—chaplain, parent, daughter, spouse, friend, pastor—erupted with such delight that I could not contain it. That day, I stumbled across one more threshold, this time a threshold that beckons the company of chaplain and young people. As we come to this threshold, those who are there with me will face many locked doors and unexpected entries—some welcome, others not. But as I look into the eyes of those whose lives I have had the privilege to enter, to accompany, I realize that my work as chaplain is to hold the door open to them as they go on their way. There is a grand vista ahead of them, along with the daunting call for our students to lead this world.

Bibliography

Buechner, Frederick. *Alphabet of Grace*. New York: HarperCollins, 1970.

———. *Wishful Thinking: A Theological ABC*. New York: Harper and Row, 1973.

Forster-Smith, Lucy. "Musings on My Ministry." *Theology Today* 41:2 (July 1984) 173–82.

Loder, Ted. *Guerrillas of Grace*. San Diego: LuraMedia, 1984.

Oliver, Ian. "In Coffin's Pulpit: Re-envisioning Protestant Religious Culture." In *College and University Chaplaincy in the 21st Century: A Multifaith Look at the Practice of Ministry on Campuses Across America*, edited by Lucy Forster-Smith, 45–60. Woodstock, VT: SkyLight Paths, 2013.

Parks, Sharon Daloz. *Big Questions, Worthy Dreams*. San Francisco: Jossey Bass, 2000.

Rich, Adrienne. "Disloyal to Civilization: Feminism, Racism, Gynophobia." In *On Lies, Secrets and Silence: Selected Prose 1966–1978*, 275–310. New York: Norton, 1979.

———. "Women and Honor: Some Notes on Lying." In *On Lies, Secrets and Silence: Selected Prose 1966–1978*, 185–94. New York: Norton, 1979.

Rilke, Rainer Maria. *Letters to a Young Poet*. New York: Random House, 1984.

Shakespeare, William. *Macbeth*. Cambridge: Cambridge University Press, 2008.